How to Lead When You Don't Know Where You're Going

How to Lead When You Don't Know Where You're Going

Leading in a Liminal Season

Rev. Susan Beaumont

An Alban Institute Book

ROWMAN & LITTLEFIELD
Lanham • Boulder • New York • London

The names of the churches in this book are fictional. Any resemblance to actual churches is purely coincidental.

Published by Rowman & Littlefield
An imprint of The Rowman & Littlefield Publishing Group, Inc.
4501 Forbes Boulevard, Suite 200, Lanham, Maryland 20706
https://rowman.com

6 Tinworth Street, London SE11 5AL, United Kingdom

British Library Cataloguing in Publication Information Available

Library of Congress Cataloging-in-Publication Data

Names: Beaumont, Susan, author.
Title: How to lead when you don't know where you're going : leading in a
    liminal season / Rev. Susan Beaumont.
Description: Lanham : Rowman & Littlefield Publishing Group, Inc., 2019. |
    Includes bibliographical references and index.
Identifiers: LCCN 2019010261 (print) | LCCN 2019981048 (ebook) | ISBN
    9781538127674 (cloth : alk. paper) | ISBN 9781538127681 (pbk. : alk.
    paper) | ISBN 9781538127698 (ebook)
Subjects: LCSH: Liminality--Religious aspects--Christianity. | Christian
    leadership. | Leadership--Religious aspects--Christianity.
Classification: LCC BR111 .B43 2019 (print) | LCC BR111 (ebook) | DDC
    253--dc23
LC record available at https://lccn.loc.gov/2019010261
LC ebook record available at https://lccn.loc.gov/2019981048

Contents

Preface

I have been consulting with congregations and their leaders for over two decades. Prior to that, I worked in corporate America, in academia, and with non-profits. I left those other institutional settings to focus exclusively on the world of congregations because church utterly fascinates me. Congregations are unique covenantal communities, often saddled with organizational dysfunction. Balancing spiritual, relational, and organizational health is challenging leadership work.

Despite my fascination with church, several years ago I found myself stymied by the ministry. Many churches and synagogues were inviting me to help with strategic planning, staff team design, board development, and performance management issues. My previous two books and my earlier affiliation with the Alban Institute established me as an expert in these areas, particularly for larger congregations. My clients valued the work I was doing with them, but I was growing increasingly frustrated. The accelerated pace of decline in the mainline church was overwhelming. Nothing in my work seemed to mitigate the loss.

More importantly, I was dismayed at the growing disconnect between the spiritual and organizational lives of congregations. As I worked with governing bodies and staff teams, it was rarely evident that I was working in a faith-based environment. Frankly, some of the work that I had done in corporate America felt more sacred than the work I was doing in churches. My clients were working in overdrive to reverse decline and improve organizational effectiveness. Few were engaging God as a partner in the striving. Increasingly, I felt that the organizational work was replacing the spiritual center of the institutions I served. Something felt remarkably off.

As an antidote to my malaise, I decided to sign up for the spiritual guidance program at the Shalem Institute. Perhaps learning the skills of spiritual direction would help me integrate my faith and work life. Perhaps a difference in me would draw forth something more sacred from my clients.

I was right on one account: I was changed by the experience. My experience at Shalem was spiritually rich and deepening. I became more centered in God, better attuned to my surroundings, and more deeply present to my clients. However, the change in me didn't translate into a change in my clients' systems. Bridging the divide between organizational and spiritual leadership was getting harder—not easier.

This is when I claimed a subtle but important vocational shift, discerning that I was called to function as a spiritual director to the *organizations* I served, not the leaders of those organizations. I wasn't certain what that meant, but the phrase "tending the soul of the institution" took hold of me and wouldn't let go. I began researching the topic but couldn't find a central organizing principle to ground the work. Helpful resources were available for developing spiritually centered leaders and for fostering individual discernment. I couldn't find much that helped leaders bridge the discernment work to their organizational leadership. What resources I did find were geared more toward business leaders, and I wondered why the world of business was generating better resources than the church on contemplative leadership.

Discovering Victor Turner's work on liminality was an important personal discovery, a key that profoundly shifted my thinking and approach. I began to understand this season of church life as a liminal era, and that began to shape my understanding of the challenges we face. Tending the soul of the institution began to make sense when viewed through the lens of liminality. Each time I introduced liminality in a client setting, something shifted for my clients as well. Leaders began framing their challenges as a liminal experience, and this seemed to unleash fresh energy, creativity, and hope.

The book you are holding in your hands is the result of five years of prayer, thinking, and teaching around this topical shift. I do not claim to have "arrived" anywhere. The ideas you will read here are still very much a work in progress. But it seems right to set the ideas into print and expand the number of partners in the conversation.

How to Lead When You Don't Know Where You're Going: Leading in a Liminal Season is meant to be a practical book of hope for tired and weary leaders who are in danger of defining this era of ministry in terms of failure or loss. This book does not attempt to describe where the church is headed. These chapters will raise many questions and provide no easy answers. You won't find five easy steps or three simple solutions to anything. There are no promises of church growth. Rather, you will be invited to stand firm in a disoriented state, learn from your mistakes, and lead despite your confusion.

The premise of this book is that traditional leadership stances and practices do not serve us well in liminal seasons. An alternative way of being and a different body of work are needed to negotiate liminality. A chapter outline will help you negotiate your way.

Chapter 1: An Introduction to Liminality: Neither Here nor There

Liminality refers to a quality of ambiguity or disorientation that occurs during transition, when a person or group of people is in between something that has ended and something else that is not yet ready to begin. Transition experiences follow a predictable pattern that involves separation, liminality, and reorientation. This chapter introduces liminality and explores the challenges and opportunities facing congregations in this liminal season.

Chapter 2: Leading with Presence: Holding Steady

The success of any leadership intervention rests upon the quality of the leader's attention to all that is unfolding—on her or his ability to remain non-anxious, to be self-reflective, and to self-differentiate personal issues from the issues of the organization. This chapter explores three spiritual shifts that help leaders respond more effectively in liminal seasons: from knowing to unknowing, from advocating to attending, and from striving to surrender.

Chapter 3: Tending the Soul of the Institution: Finding Soul in Place

The soul is the authentic and truest self of the organization, the source of its divine calling and character, and the protector of institutional integrity. In liminal seasons we rely upon the soul of the institution to guide our leadership choices and our learning. This chapter explores the quality of soul in an institution and introduces four types of organizational work that are appropriate for soul-tending: deepening communal discernment, shaping institutional memory, clarifying organizational purpose, and engaging emergence.

Chapter 4: Deepening Group Discernment: Seeing What God Is Up To

Discernment is an attentiveness to God that, over time, develops into a sense of God's intention. In communal discernment, we move beyond the personal to see what God is doing within the collective whole. This chapter explores the challenge of working with discernment in communal settings during times of high anxiety and uncertainty.

Chapter 5: Shaping Institutional Memory: Tell Me Our Story

In liminal seasons we have clarity only about our past. This condition can invite an unhealthy relationship with the past. The temptation is to glamorize our glory eras. We create thin narratives about how wonderful things were back then. Or we truncate our memories to block out experiences of pain and shame. Memory shaping helps the organization rightly remember stories from the past, so that those stories teach important values for the present and shape a hope-filled future.

Chapter 6: Clarifying Purpose: Who Do We Choose to Be?

Determining what is ours to do is at the heart of the liminal experience. Amid disruption and disorientation, the leader must help the organization determine what is worth preserving, what can be released, and what must be adapted. This requires forming a proximate purpose centered around four basic questions: Who are we? Who are we here to serve? What do we stand for? What is God calling us to do or become next?

Chapter 7: Engaging Emergence: Are We There Yet?

Eventually, liminality will find resolution. The process by which this happens is known as emergence. Reorientation will occur; it is the natural order of things for coherence to emerge out of chaos. Emergence is naturally leaderless activity. The leader can't manage the process, but the leader can nurture a climate of disruption, innovation, learning, and risk-taking, supporting the emergence of new order as it manifests.

I am not naïve. I do not believe that approaching this era of church life through the lens of liminality will resolve many of our issues. I do believe it invites us to eliminate the false divide between organizational and spiritual leadership. I do believe it beckons us to engage God more authentically in our work and to approach our ministry with a greater sense of awe and joy.

Many stories of leaders and congregations appear in the pages that follow. The stories are all truthful, in that the problems and challenges really happened in congregations I have had the pleasure of knowing. However, it is important to note that every story you will read is a fictionalized telling of the truth. Names, locations, and key identifiers have been changed to protect the identity of the congregations. Stories have been conflated or simplified to better illustrate a teaching point. Sometimes, the processes described aren't what a congregation really did, but what I hoped they might do. Often, the best course of action isn't evident at the time of decision-making, and I wrote with the privilege of hindsight, able to reflect on what a better alternative might have been. I am forever grateful to the many congregations and leaders whose stories are adapted here, and to the many other clients whose leadership challenges form the bedrock of my perspective.

I owe a debt of gratitude to so many people who have served as conversation and editorial partners in this work. I couldn't possibly name all the voices that have helped to shape this product. However, the following individuals were particularly instrumental in helping me clarify my thinking and sharpen the work.

My developmental editor, Beth Gaede, spoke truth into this work more times than I can count. Beth encouraged my spirit in the early days when I wasn't even sure this should be a book. She challenged me when the work was shoddy and shored me up on days when I was ready to abandon the effort.

My publishing partners at Rowman & Littlefield carefully tended the manuscript through to its final release. I am grateful to Rolf Janke for recognizing the value in the initial proposal, and to Chris Fischer for dealing with my ongoing challenges around comma placement and capitalization.

Mostly, I want to thank the following individuals who serve as ongoing spiritual guides in my life. These are the people who sustain me with prayer, encouragement, and their unflagging belief in the ideas presented in these chapters: Tom Allen, Mary O'Connell, Marjorie Wilhelmi, Kate Thoresen, Larry Peers, Alice Mann, Susan Nienaber, Debra Griest, Liz Stewart, and Patricia D'Auria, I am blessed by your support and delighted that you are with me on this journey.

Chapter One

An Introduction to Liminality

Neither Here nor There

There is a sweet spot between the known and the unknown where originality happens; the key is to be able to linger there without panicking.
—Ed Catmull (Pixar)

Pastor Jon is brand new to his congregation. He is a bright young leader, high on potential but with no previous experience as a senior pastor. The congregation is a little edgy about Jon's leadership. Will he have the skills and maturity to lead this congregation? Members are eager for Jon to prove himself early on, so that they can relax and feel confident about their decision to call him.

Jon is only too eager to please. He wants to do something new, bold, and brilliant to quell their anxiety, as well as his own. The problem is that the new thing is not yet apparent—even to Jon. Lots of great ideas abound, but leaders have not reached consensus about a way forward, at least not yet. Jon and the congregation are still discovering one another. They are in liminal space, stuck at a threshold between an ending and a new beginning.

Neither Jon nor his congregation are keen about being in this space. Liminality fuels ambiguity and disorientation. The people would rather go back to the comfort of the old status quo they enjoyed with their previous leader or make a dramatic leap forward. They look to their new leader to resolve their discomfort, and they wonder if his hesitancy to lead decisively is a sign of weakness.

A liminal organization needs to unlearn old behaviors, challenge the status quo, experiment, take risks, and learn. To do these things Jon will have to employ leadership skills that are different from the skill set that got him hired. Jon will need to demonstrate a leadership presence that is both deeply spiritual and organizationally savvy. He will need to tend the soul of the institution, as well as care for the souls in the institution.

Organizational life is full of liminal experiences—seasons where something has ended, but a new thing has not yet begun. Seasons where watching and waiting can be difficult, overplanning can be futile, and it simply isn't helpful to pretend that we understand what happens next.

Liminal seasons are challenging, disorienting, and unsettling. We strive to move forward with purpose and certainty. Instead, we feel as though we are trudging through mud, moving away from something comfortable and known, toward something that can't yet be known.

Liminal seasons are also exciting and innovative. The promise of a new beginning unleashes creative energy, potential, and passion. All truly great innovations are incubated in liminality. God's greatest work occurs in liminal space.

THE LIMINAL EXPERIENCE

While writing this text, I became a grandparent for the first time. So much of the grandparenting experience has been rich and wonderful, but one of the most remarkable things has been watching Katie and Chris become parents. Baby Ethan's arrival marked a significant change in their lives. One day they were a couple; the next day they were a family. However, the transition into parenthood didn't correspond exactly with the moment of birth. Katie and Chris grew into their identity as parents over a long season that began before pregnancy and continued well after the baby was born.

Pregnancy was an active time of waiting and planning. For months Katie and Chris lived in this liminal state, no longer a newlywed couple, but not yet parents. For nine months, the couple prepared for the arrival of the baby. They read books. They received baby gifts. They took birthing classes. They let go of their fourth-floor walk-up apartment in the city and moved to a three-bedroom home in the suburbs. They bought their first car.

Katie and Chris prepared, but no book or class could fully ready the couple for the overwhelming real-life experience of parenting: the awe and fear of childbirth, their indescribable love of this child, the total exhaustion of sleepless nights. A couple can prepare, but they can't know what they don't know. Until after the baby arrives.

All significant transitional experiences, like becoming parents, follow a predictable three-part process. Something comes to an end. There is an in-between season marked by disorientation, disidentification, and disengagement. Finally, and often after a very long and painful struggle, something new emerges.

1. Separation: A period in which a person, group, or social order is stripped of the identity and status that previously defined it.
2. Liminal Period: A disorienting period of non-structure or anti-structure that opens new possibilities no longer based on old status or power hierarchies. New identities are explored, and new possibilities are considered.
3. Reorientation: A reforming period in which the person, group, or social order adopts a new identity, is granted new status, and designs new structures more appropriately suited to the emerging identity.

The middle, or liminal, period is the focus of this book, because it is fraught with both opportunity and danger. The liminal period can be an incredibly freeing season in which old structures are released, new identities and possibilities are explored, and power is reassigned. It is also a troubling time during which people are subject to the lure of tricksters. Leaders and followers may be tempted down false pathways that serve no useful purpose.

The natural human response is to resist liminality and to strive backward to the old familiar identity, or forward to the unknown identity. The ambiguity and disorientation are at times so heightened that the very work required to move forward becomes impossible to engage.

The Israelites weren't in the wilderness very long before they began grumbling about how nice it had been back in Egypt, where things were at least predictable and stomachs were full. They alternated between begging Moses to go back and demanding to know how quickly they might move forward.

The Israelites endured a lengthy liminal era during which they struggled to leave behind their identity as slaves. They discovered a new identity and social structure better suited for a free and chosen people. Reorientation occurred as they settled into the promised land some forty years later.

ALREADY AND NOT YET

The Judeo-Christian story is filled with liminal experiences. Our scriptures tell stories of characters who wander in and out of liminal times and spaces, being shaped further into the likeness of God through the power of liminality.

Adam and Eve's fall from grace in the Garden of Eden sets up the biblical story as one large liminal experience. Humankind leaves the garden and begins an ongoing journey toward redemption and salvation.

Noah endures the flood. All of humanity, except for his family, is left behind. He enters a liminal season played out within the confines of an ark, followed by a reorientation to new life atop Mount Ararat.

Ruth gives up her identity as a Moabite. Attaching herself to Naomi, Ruth moves to Judah, leaving her family of origin behind. After a prolonged period of wandering and not belonging, Ruth meets and marries Boaz. She eventually becomes the great grandmother of King David and provides an important link in the lineage of Jesus.

Joseph is thrown into a pit, signifying an end to his smug identity as the favored son. His time as an indentured servant in Egypt is a liminal testing ground that eventually gives birth to a new identity as dream interpreter, royal advisor, and eventual redeemer of his people.

Abraham, Sarah, Jacob, and Job each have a liminal tale to tell. Each biblical journey is a venturing forth: an ending, followed by a disorienting season of transition, and finally a reorientation to something new that is substantially different from what was left behind. Clearly, God works with liminality. Through liminal experiences human beings are transformed and brought into deeper relationship with God.

In the New Testament, Jesus begins his ministry in liminal space. Rising out of the baptismal waters Jesus enters the desert for a period of forty days and nights, a liminal pilgrimage during which his new identity is formed and tested. His return from the wilderness signals entry into a new life as teacher, healer, and savior.

The apostle Paul enters a liminal period quite suddenly when he is struck by a blinding light on the road to Damascus. In a moment he is separated from his old identity, no longer the one breathing threats and murder against the followers of Jesus. Paul emerges from his blindness reoriented as an instrument of God, chosen to bring the good news of Jesus to the Gentiles.

The Christian story is, by design, an invitation into liminality. The hoped-for reign of God is already inaugurated in the figure of Jesus Christ, but not yet complete. We embrace an understanding of our eternal lives as liminally suspended until the final return of Christ. We have already been redeemed, but the fulfillment of that redemption will not be complete until the end times when Christ returns. Our theology frames an identity for us of semi-permanent liminality.

Franciscan father and author Richard Rohr describes God's use of liminal experience in this way:

> All transformation takes place here. We have to allow ourselves to be drawn out of "business as usual" and remain patiently on the "threshold" (limen, in Latin) where we are betwixt and between the familiar and the completely unknown. There alone is our old world left behind, while we are not yet sure of the new existence. That's a good space where genuine newness can begin. Get there often and stay as long as you can by whatever means possible. It's the realm where God can best get at us because our false certitudes are finally out of the way. This is the sacred space where the old world is able to fall apart, and a bigger world is revealed. If we don't encounter liminal space in our

lives, we start idealizing normalcy. The threshold is God's waiting room. Here we are taught openness and patience as we come to expect an appointment with the divine Doctor. [1]

Why then are we resistant to living in a liminal state? Isn't it clear that God is working on us and with us in liminal seasons? Why is the disorientation that we experience so intolerable? Why do we stand outside of our own story and pray for liminality to end, when the liminality is itself an invitation to transformation?

Our resistance stems from the fact that liminality always begins with an ending, an experience of loss. And humankind resists loss. We also resist the unknowing inherent in "not yet"—the loss of control over our own destiny.

ORIGINS OF THE TERM

The words liminal and liminality are both derived from the Latin *limen*, meaning a threshold; that is, the bottom part of a doorway that must be crossed when entering a building. In Latin, *limen* referred to the stone placed on the threshold of a door that physically had to be mounted to cross from one space into another. [2]

The Roman god Janus characterizes the liminal experience. Janus is the god of beginnings, gates, transitions, time, doorways, passages, and endings. He is usually depicted as having two faces, as he looks to the future and to the past.

A corollary concept is the Greek *herma*, a stone deposited on borderlines to mark the limit or boundary of a place. The Greek god Hermes takes his name from the root of this Greek word. Hermes is widely associated with ambivalence. He is a translator between languages, messenger, and a guide of souls. He is also a liar, a thief, and a trickster in each of these roles. [3]

Our modern use of the term "liminality" was coined in the field of anthropology in 1909 by Arnold Van Gennep in his seminal work *Les rites de passage*. Van Gennep created the term to talk about rituals in small-scale societies, rituals such as coming of age, anointing tribal leadership, and marriage. Van Gennep claimed that such rituals exist in every culture. These rituals or rites follow a three-fold sequential structure, which he identified as preliminal, liminal, and postliminal. [4]

An initiate, the person undergoing the ritual, is stripped of the social status that he or she possessed before the ritual, inducted into a liminal period of transition, and finally granted new status and reoriented into society. A young boy coming of age is separated from his mother and the community, sent into the wilderness alone on a quest to prove his manhood, welcomed back into the community, and marked in some way to signify his manhood. During the liminal period, the initiand lives outside of his normal environment. The initiand is brought to question himself and the old social order through a series of rituals that involve separation and experiences of pain. During liminality the initiate is meant to feel nameless, spatio-temporally dislocated, and socially adrift. The absence of identity makes room for the inner transformation, preparing the initiand for entry into a new social order upon his return.[5]

Van Gennep's work on liminality remained obscure until the late 1960s, when it was popularized by the writing of anthropologist Victor Turner. Turner borrowed the term liminality and expanded its usage, beyond its application in ritual settings. Turner applied liminality more broadly to the social, political, and behavioral sciences. Turner's work focused exclusively on the middle stage of passage—the transitional or liminal stage. He described it this way: "Liminality may perhaps be regarded as the Nay to all positive structural assertions, but as in some sense the source of them all, and more than that, as a realm of pure possibility whence novel configurations of ideas and relations may arise."[6]

FORMS OF LIMINALITY

Liminality can describe the evolving state of an individual, place, organization, or institution—anything stuck in the neutral space between an ending and a new beginning. Liminality can also be understood relative to physical spaces and periods of time. In fact, liminality can describe the disorientation of an entire era or civilization.[7]

Consider the airport as an example of liminal space, a sort of non-space. People assemble in airports on their way to and from other places. The airport is a critical connecting point, but it is not a destination for anyone, except perhaps for the people who work there. When we are in the airport, we are neither here nor there, and we operate with a different set of behaviors than would be acceptable at home, work, or play.

As a frequent traveler, I am powerfully aware of the disorientation I feel in airports and on airplanes. I respond to the disorientation with a sense of urgency once I pass through the TSA checkpoint. I pick up my pace and move quickly, even on days when I have hours to burn before my flight is scheduled to leave.

I am also aware of how personally detached I become from everyone around me. I rarely engage in conversation, even when I spend several hours in physical contact with the person next to me on the plane, the person with whom I share an armrest or leg space. This is behavior that I would never find acceptable in another context, but in this liminal space I operate by different rules.

I also adopt an attitude of detached indifference concerning changes in gates and travel times, recognizing that I have no control and simply must yield, however my day unfolds. In most other situations I am deeply invested in managing my schedule and my environment to produce desired outcomes. When I enter the airport, I embrace the zone between worlds, the place over which I have no control.

Liminality also applies to the dimension of time. Twilight is a daily liminal experience demarking the boundary between day and night. New Year's Day is an annual liminal time, a powerful boundary marking the passage of one year to the next, between our old selves and the possibility of something yet undiscovered.

Most of the liminal experiences described so far can be resolved in relatively short time frames. In a matter of hours, days, or months we can move through a separation, a liminal period, and reorientation. Sometimes, liminality takes decades, generations, or even centuries to resolve. When an entire civilization or society moves into a prolonged liminal state, we call this a liminal epoch. Many believe that civilization is in a liminal epoch right now. Certainly, the Church is liminal.

CONGREGATIONS AND LIMINALITY

Congregations regularly experience liminal seasons. The interim time between established pastorates. The beginning of a new pastorate, when consensus about the way forward is still forming. The end of a building project when leaders are spent, and no one knows what is being called forth from the new space. Following the completion of a strategic plan, when leaders are left wondering where the next big idea will come from. The death of a matriarch or patriarch. Liminal seasons are threshold experiences where the continuity of tradition is called into question, and uncertainty about the future fuels doubt.

During liminal seasons we stand on both sides of a threshold. We have one foot rooted in something that is not yet over, whereas the other foot is planted in a thing not yet defined, something not yet ready to begin. Our old operating structures may no longer work. Our denominational polity, our governing board and committee structures, our staffing arrangement—all were suited for conditions that have evolved. Our strategic identities—who we are, who we serve, and what we feel called to do or become—were shaped by old experiences. We may no longer be served well by these outdated constructs, but we aren't certain what we need next.

Liminal seasons are not the same as seasons of intentional change management. During change management, leaders know where they stand and where they are headed. In change management, the leader must build consen-

sus, overcome resistance, and remove obstacles that stand in the way of a
desired future. During liminal seasons, our destination is not yet clear. The
leader must keep the people moving forward, but the endpoint is fuzzy.
Liminal seasons require us to build the bridge as we walk on it.

THIS LIMINAL EPOCH

Phyllis Tickle wrote about this liminal era in her ground-breaking work *The
Great Emergence: How Christianity Is Changing and Why*. Tickle characterized this current era of Church as a giant rummage sale, akin to the Great
Reformation and the Great Schism. Tickle argues that the Church endures a
great upheaval like this one every five hundred years.[8]

Krista Tippett, religious journalist and host of the radio show "On Being,"
describes our present liminal era as a spiritual revolution, marked by profound spiritual curiosity, deep theological engagement, and a reawakening of
a mystery that embraces science. Tippett compares this period to the out-
break of early monasticism in the sixth century and the movement of the
desert fathers and mothers in the first centuries of Christianity.[9]

Church historian Diana Butler Bass takes a different approach to describing this epoch. In *Grounded*, Butler Bass describes a spiritual upheaval flowing from the ending of our three-tiered understanding of the universe, with
God in heaven, humanity here on earth, and the dreaded underworld of death.
In its place we are discovering a God that is grounded, present within and
among us. The grounded God is in relationship with space and time and
nature, the love that connects and creates all things. The Church is discovering new pathways that enfold the mundane and the sacred, finding a God that
is simultaneously other worldly, mystical, and near.[10]

Butler Bass asserts that the institutional Church is losing its efficacy, and
its membership, because people are experiencing too great a distance between the old structures of the Church and their lived experience of this
richer understanding of God. Something in the Church must be stripped
away, and the Church must reorient itself in profound ways if it is going to
remain relevant in this new world order. In the meantime, as we are discovering our way forward, we are in liminal space.

Regardless of how we characterize this epoch, one thing is clear. We are
engaged in a transformation, the outcome of which is presently unknowable.
The basic models and processes that define Church are being deconstructed.
They are crumbling around us. Some new ways are emerging, but we do not
yet know what the new world order will be, what forms of institutional
church, if any, will remain. We are surrounded by prophetic voices trying to
point a way forward, but it is not yet clear which pathways we should follow
and which we should be wary of. And we are tired. It is exhausting trying to

keep the old structures intact, managing the anxiety of the transition, and making space for the birth of the new thing—all at the same time.

Many in church leadership began their ministry when the old order held sway. They have clear memories of an institutional church that worked well. Some church leaders have only dim memories of those times from childhood. And still others know only the experience of liminality, like the Israelites born in exile who lived their entire lives separated from temple life in Jerusalem, unmoored from the historical center of their tradition.

THE COLLAPSE OF ORDER

People and organizations can tolerate a certain amount of ambiguity in the natural order of things. Our identity, our structures, and our processes can accommodate disorientation in measured doses. However, when too many aspects of our lives become simultaneously ambiguous we lose our ability to cope. We bump up against our liminal tolerance.

The greater the number and degree of liminal factors, the greater the experience of liminality. Katie and Chris, introduced earlier in this chapter, ultimately coped well with their move to the suburbs and the arrival of a new baby. However, if we added the loss of a job and/or a major health event into the equation, the young family would likely experience a level of stress and disorientation beyond their coping limits.

Similarly, organizations encounter liminal tolerance. St. Luke's Church, located in a transient, professional community, offers an example. Industry executives transfer in and out of the area frequently and the average tenure of church members is fewer than seven years. The congregation is accustomed to low-level continuous change.

But now, we add in a major building campaign. The sanctuary is under renovation and the congregation is worshiping in rotating locations around the neighboring community. Then the denomination introduces an initiative on same-sex marriage that the congregation must vote upon in the next six months. The congregation is conflicted about its stance on this issue.

It is not surprising to learn that many of the leadership structures of the church are disintegrating. The senior pastor's leadership is being called into question. Triangulated gossip is running rampant in the church. People who have been sitting on the margins of the congregation are suddenly stepping into leadership roles and long-tenured leaders are leaving. The congregation is in a heightened liminal state, and congregants are feeling extremely anxious.

We approach a condition known as "pure liminality," when temporal and spatial personal, group, and, societal forces all move into a liminal state at the same time.[11] When this occurs, the disorientation is severe, and the existing infrastructures fail to hold. Structure gives way to anti-structure, and organizations and institutions begin to collapse. Many would argue that the mainline church is approaching pure liminality.

Beginning with an Ending

Entry into a liminal state always begins with the collapse of order. Something comes to an end: an identity, a program, a structure, or a process.

Our Savior's Church has long been known for excellence in children's ministry. For generations, the church prided itself on helping families raise up children in faith. The number of children in the church began declining over a decade ago. There are no longer enough young children to maintain an active nursery or preschool program. The youth program has lost much of its vitality and will not be viable for much longer. The demographics of the community have changed and few families with young children live within a five-mile radius of the church.

Our Savior's is struggling with its disintegrating programs and identity: If we no longer excel at children's and youth ministry, then who are we and why should we exist? Some people are leaving in response to the disorientation. Others are simply refusing to serve as volunteers. Still others are blaming the pastor for not attracting more families with young children.

In some instances, liminality emerges through the slow death of systems or structures that have outlived their usefulness. A congregation has been limping along with an ineffective governance structure designed for a much larger congregation. The committee structure is too cumbersome to negotiate. Communication patterns within the congregation break down, and decision-making grounds to a halt. Leaders resist downsizing because they don't want to acknowledge that their decline is permanent. "Maybe if we just wait long enough, we will grow again and work more effectively with our cumbersome structure."

Cracks begin to appear in the old structure. The congregation can't recruit enough leaders to staff their oversized governing board. They miss out on an important opportunity in the community because it takes them too long to decide if they will participate. Eventually, through the cracks of a broken structure leaders begin to see glimmers of something else wanting to emerge—a leaner, nimbler structure. But first, the old thing must die. Something that once held value ceases to provide safety, security, identity, or meaning.

Business consultant William Bridges is well known for his book *Managing Transitions: Making the Most of Change*. Bridges draws a distinction between change and transition. Change is situational and depends upon the arrival of something new: moving to a new site, calling a new leader, assigning new team roles, adopting the new policy. In contrast, transition is the psychological process people go through to come to terms with the change. Transition depends upon the ending of what was: saying goodbye to the old building, letting the old leader go, releasing the identity attached to the old roles. The starting point for any kind of transition, Bridges tells us, is not the outcome you are moving toward, but the ending that you must make to leave the old situation behind. [12]

For example, a change occurs on the day a pastor walks out the door and begins her retirement. But the full transition work, the psychological and spiritual work of letting go of that pastor, began well before the retirement date and extends for a period of years beyond the arrival of the new pastor. The congregation enters a long period of liminality during which the people learn to let go of identities and behaviors held together by the ex-leader's presence. A new pastor may arrive, but the congregation remains in liminal space until the full transition occurs, until collapse of the old identity is allowed.

In the meantime, leaders must manage the anxiety related to the loss. Too much anxiety freezes people into inactivity or unleashes unmanageable levels of conflict. Not enough anxiety and people don't feel the need to let go. The right level of anxiety invites followers to adapt, to leave the comfort of what was and enter a liminal state.

International consultants Ronald Heifetz, Marty Linsky, and Alexander Grashow call this type of work adaptive leadership. The core of adaptive leadership is regulating the pace of loss that people experience—to keep people from bumping up against their liminal tolerance limit. A leader doesn't create or eliminate loss. Rather, he or she tries to control the pace at which people experience the loss. He or she protects people from experiencing too much of the loss at one time. In this way the organization continues its adaptive work and eventually moves toward reorientation. [13]

Entering the Liminal State

As we embrace our losses and recognize our endings we move tentatively into the undifferentiated middle state of transition, liminality. Liminality is simultaneously dangerous, alluring, and sacred.

Let's talk about the danger first. A liminal season or space is highly uncertain because the structures that define "normal" have crumbled. Social hierarchies are temporarily dissolved. Some people who never held a position of leadership in the church move into the power center, and some who used to wield considerable power step to the sidelines. This disorientation carries with it a sense of anguish and existential fear; it involves facing into a void, the collapse of order and status as we have come to understand it. The continuity of our tradition is called into question. We become nameless; if we are no longer that, then who are we? Or whose are we?

As dangerous as a liminal state may feel, it is also alluring. The suddenly malleable situation invites experimentation and risk-taking. We are free to question traditions, which also invites originality, generativity, and creativity. We may also grow in our sense of agency, free to discover and design a future unencumbered by the past.

William Bridges describes the liminal season in an organizational setting as "The Neutral Zone":

> Just when you've decided that the hardest part of managing transition is getting people to let go of the old ways, you enter a state of affairs in which neither the old ways nor the new ways work satisfactorily. People are caught between the demands of conflicting systems. . . . If this phase lasted only a short time, you could just wait for it to pass. But when the change is deep and far-reaching, this time between the old identity and the new can stretch out for months, even years. This is a time when you've let go of one trapeze with the faith that the new trapeze is on its way. In the meantime, there's nothing to hold on to.[14]

In organizational settings, predictable behaviors emerge in the neutral space:[15]

- Anxiety rises; motivation falls. People question their attachment to the organization or the cause. They wonder if they want to continue the relationship.
- Attendance drops off. Some people stop attending altogether, planning to take a break until the liminal season is over. Others attend but with less frequency, deciding that this is a good time to pull back, take a bit of a break, and wait to see what emerges next. The detachment of some places additional stress on others who find they must pick up the slack of those taking a breather.
- Old weaknesses, long patched over or compensated for, reemerge in full bloom. Old conflict issues reemerge.
- Personnel are overloaded. Signals about what is important are mixed, and systems are in flux and therefore unreliable. It takes more effort to accomplish everything, even the most mundane daily tasks.
- People in the organization are easily polarized between those who want to rush forward into the new thing and those who long to return to the old familiar ways.

The primary work in leading people through the liminal phase is to normalize the experience and to frame/define the season as acceptable and even desirable. One of the most difficult aspects of liminality is that people don't understand it and they tend to think of it as undesirable and aberrant.

People often frame the liminal experience as organizational failure, believing it occurs because leaders aren't doing what they are supposed to be doing, which is to keep followers happy and safe. People expect to move in a straight line from the old things to the new, and the waiting and confusion feels meaningless or counter-productive. An effective leader will teach people about the importance and value of a liminal season, why they are feeling the way they are feeling, and what they can do with their anxiety. [16]

The leader may or may not have clarity about what lies on the other side of liminality. Those being led see only the losses they are being asked to sustain. The effective leader invites the people to examine and adapt attitudes, values, assumptions, and behaviors—to understand the loss as something productive. Without letting go, the people cannot make the adaptive leap into reorientation. [17]

Kathryn is the pastor of a congregation that has been in decline for some time. The congregation offers two worship experiences on Sunday morning. Neither worship service feels vibrant. The physical space feels empty. The church has only enough resources to provide Sunday school at one of the services. The church can't recruit enough musical volunteers to ensure quality music at both services. Kathryn knows that the congregation needs to move to one service.

This season in Kathryn's congregation isn't simply about deciding how to combine two worship services into one. That's an easy "problem" to solve. Kathryn can figure out the logistics of that quite easily. The real challenge is in helping the congregation adapt its self-image. The image of a large and resource-rich congregation that can sustain multiple services is dead. The congregation must embrace a new and more realistic image of themselves as a mid-sized church with resource limitations. Some people will leave the congregation over this loss of image. They valued being part of a church with a large, resource-rich identity. Some will reject Kathryn as a leader because they hold her responsible for the decline. If Kathryn were a "good" leader, they might argue, she would have found a way to build attendance and keep both services.

Kathryn's job during this liminal period of adjustment is to keep the people focused on their adaptive work: What size congregation are we? What are we called to do or become in this season? How then shall we worship? She must resist her own impulses to protect them from disappointment. She must endure the beating that her own ego will take as she manages this downsizing. She must resist telling them that nothing is really changing—because a huge transition *is* taking place.

Kathryn cannot do this adaptive work on behalf of the congregation. She can coordinate the actual combination of services, but she can't make the people engage the transition work. She can invite them to it. Kathryn needs to provoke disorientation. But she also needs to monitor anxiety so that the disorientation doesn't become too intense.

Here is what Kathryn can do as she seeks to intensify the disorientation. [18] She can:

- Draw attention to the tough unresolved questions. "What are we doing when we gather for worship? Does our mission or purpose suggest that we ought to have more than one worship experience weekly?"
- Give people more responsibility than they are comfortable with. "Why don't you go out and assess the worship experiences of several neighboring congregations? Come back and report on your observations."
- Bring conflicts to the surface rather than diminishing them. "The 10:30 worship service provides 70 percent of the pledges that support our operating budget. The 8:30 service provides only 30 percent but uses more than half of our worship budget. Should these budget patterns inform our decision?"
- Name the dynamics in the room to illustrate some of the issues facing the group. "If we eliminate the 8:30 service we may disenfranchise a core group of our more senior members. Are we prepared to help them cope with their disorientation?"

At times, Kathryn may need to cool things down a bit when the disorientation gets too intense. She may engage in different leadership behaviors to quiet things down and keep people in a productive zone of disequilibrium, so that they can engage the adaptive work at hand. She might:

- Address aspects of the problem that are easily solvable. Take care of some of the low-hanging fruit. Active problem solving always calms people down. "Let's contact the city and see what we can do to resolve our problems with street parking on Sunday mornings. This will pave the way for higher worship attendance if we choose to consolidate our worship experiences."
- Create a timeline and a plan for moving forward. "Can we all agree that we will work toward a joint decision by January 31? Let's generate a list of all the things that have to be resolved before we can consider merging the two services."
- Temporarily reclaim responsibility for some of the tough issues. "I will host a listening session for the senior adult members of our community to hear what they have to say about our options."
- Slow down the process of challenging norms and expectations. "Why don't we take a break on this conversation during the season of Advent and Christmas?"

There are moments when Kathryn will provoke and challenge. Other moments when she will cajole and comfort. She will always be drawing the people back to who they are, who they serve, and what God is asking of them. This is the work of the liminal stage.

Encountering Communitas

In the liminal period, something marvelous and transforming can occur. Communitas might emerge. And that has the potential to change everything and everyone.

Communitas is a Latin noun referring to an unstructured community in which people are equal. It also describes the very spirit of the community itself.[19] Victor Turner adopted this term to talk about what happens when the old identity and structures die. Turner was intentional about use of this term, as opposed to the word community. He wanted to signify a state of relationship, over and above a place of common living.

In communitas, a sense of common humanity emerges in which all members are experienced as equals. Old hierarchies dissolve or are ignored. A sense of fellowship, spontaneity, and warmth emerges within newly undifferentiated social relationships; a new ethos of interrelatedness springs forth.

A common example of this occurs within groups bound together on a mission trip or pilgrimage. At the onset of the trip, members of the community may be strongly invested in the social hierarchies that order their daily lives. Pilgrims at the outset of a journey often introduce themselves to one another according to what they do, where they live, and the accomplishments of their lives.

As the journey gets underway, those social constructs disintegrate. The sojourners become co-workers on mission, fellow pilgrims in a shared sacred space. Ego identities eventually dissolve. Members of different social classes, ages, and occupations begin to interact as equals. The collapse of traditional hierarchy allows each group member to form relationships more spontaneously, unencumbered by traditional rules of interaction.

Monastic communities seek to institutionalize the state of communitas. Bound together in poverty, and by obedience and disciplines of prayer and work, the community seeks to remain in a state of permanent liminality by embracing communitas. Every member of the community is stripped of ego, cutting across previous social distinctions, bonded only by the rules of the order.

In communitas we are free to experiment and learn. Unencumbered by old expectations and assumptions about how the community is meant to work, we discover a new way of being. Creativity, compassion, daring, and curiosity emerge. Pride, cynicism, arrogance, and callousness drop away. We discover ourselves fully alive and more open to divine encounters.

The early years of wilderness wandering by the Israelites were marked by communitas and characterized by palpable divine encounters. The old identity of an enslaved people was stripped away and a new identity as God's chosen people took hold. God showed up visibly and powerfully in the transition. The Israelites experienced dramatic plagues and the parting of the Red Sea. Scripture describes a pillar of cloud that led the people by day and a pillar of fire that marked the way at night. Moses had direct encounters with God. His physical appearance was transformed on mystical mountaintops. There was nothing subtle about God's leadership in this season.

The Celtic Christian tradition teaches us about thin places. A thin place is where the material realm is only thinly separated from the spiritual; where the eternal is seeping through the physical; where shafts of divine light penetrate the thin veil that divides heaven from earth. [20]

Liminal seasons are thin spaces, where the presence of the divine is palpable. Liminal seasons are ripe opportunities for communities of faith to deepen their practices of group discernment, to watch for the movement of God.

Woodside Church struggled for decades to reverse numerical decline. Pastor Matt named the awful truth: they were going to have to sell the building and likely close the congregation. The prospect of closure unhinged something in the congregants. Several key leaders who had been protecting the old identity decided to leave. Their departure freed others to behave differently. Those who remained let go of their old identity as a one-time flagship church of the denomination. All the debates and conflict about the future of the church simply fell away. The community began to delight in itself as a group of fellow spiritual travelers, aware that very soon they would likely find their way to other congregations.

A remarkable thing happened at Woodside as they embraced their likely demise. When the pretense, ego, and struggle dropped away, communitas emerged. The voice of people with money no longer mattered more than the voices of those without. Long-time leaders held no more sway in decision-making than newer members. The power of the pastor wasn't any greater than the power of any other individual in the congregation. People turned more easily to prayer and began to sense something new emerging. Leaders opened themselves to a potential partnership with another congregation in need of a building.

Eventually, the two churches merged into a single entity. The possibility of the merger only became apparent after communitas arrived. Woodside eventually gifted its building to the newly combined entity, something it never would have considered in earlier times. The merger partner brought resources to renovate and revitalize the building. To embrace the merger, both congregations had to swallow ego and pride. Both had to embrace egalitarian ownership of the new thing.

The Dark Side of Liminality — The Trickster

Liminality also has a dangerous side. When old structures, policies, and procedures are left behind, an organization is remarkably susceptible to false leaders and prophets.

Victor Turner personified this danger when he coined the term "the trickster"—dangerous figures who look like charismatic leaders but are incapable of living well in community. Tricksters promote confusion and chaos by sowing discord. The trickster is masterful at pitting people against one another. People confuse the energy of the trickster with leadership direction. Tricksters cannot trust or be trusted. They are incapable of giving and sharing or participating well in a democratic process. Their behaviors are almost always self-serving, and they lack deep commitments to the welfare of the organization.[21]

First Community Church was managing a pastoral transition. A new senior pastor had just begun when Michael was called as one of three associate pastors. The chaos began almost immediately upon Michael's arrival. Michael proclaimed himself a change agent; he had come to fix the congregation. He told others that he had been hired as the number two clergy leader, even though the organizational chart clearly showed him on equal footing with the two other associates.

Michael began pitting staff members against one another. He isolated every member of the team by telling each that he was their only ally. Michael shared "secret" insights with team members, telling them that they were not valued by the new senior minister. He was masterful at intuiting the deepest fears of staff members and fueling those fears. He created triangulated communication patterns so that staff members stopped interacting directly. They closed their doors and began vetting their frustrations with like-minded allies instead of talking directly with one another.

After nine months of this behavior, a previously healthy team had degenerated into a mess of strained and broken relationships. Trust among team members was gone. Some began questioning the leadership capabilities of the new senior minister. Why was he allowing Michael to act out so?

Fortunately, the senior minister worked in conjunction with the personnel committee to address Michael's dysfunction. Once new systems of accountability were put into place Michael voluntarily chose to leave. He claimed that the dysfunction in the system made his role impossible. Michael was losing his ability to manipulate others and he knew it.

Tricksters are attracted to the chaos in liminal seasons. In transitional situations people have difficulty with rational thinking. Instability produces a naturally stressful, emotive, and reactive environment. People look around for someone to follow, for someone who can establish normalcy. Enter the trickster.

Tricksters are great imitators of normalcy. In organizations they are capable of mimicking core managerial and leadership behaviors that people value, enough to initially convince others they are trustworthy. However, the trickster is not at all interested in resolving liminality or stabilizing disorientation, because the trickster thrives on it.

The effective leader must limit the impact of a trickster and return functionality stolen by the trickster. No easy task. In short, this requires a leadership presence that is wise as the serpent and gentle as the dove (Matthew 10:16). More will be said about this kind of presence in chapter 2.

Readiness for a New Beginning

The third and final stage of a liminal transition is reorientation, a reforming period in which the person, group, or social order adopts a new status and structures more appropriately suited to an emerging identity. The journey is consummated here.

A new beginning doesn't happen according to schedule or plan. The merger is technically complete, the new worship service has begun, the new building is open, the strategic plan is well underway, but we still find ourselves suspended in a liminal state.

We may be able to describe the end of what was, embrace our losses, and name our challenges. It doesn't mean that we are ready to create a new organizational approach for a new day.

The thirteenth chapter of Numbers tells the story of a liminal community not yet ready for a new beginning. God vows to deliver the Israelites to the promised land, and their belief in the land sustains them through a long liminal season of wandering in the desert. Finally, God brings the people to the edge of Canaan. Moses sends in spies to check out the land. Some of the spies come back with a favorable report about a land flowing with milk and honey. Another group comes back with a report of giants who occupy the land and an admonition that the Israelites are mere grasshoppers by comparison. The people choose to listen to the negative report about the giants, rather than believe in the positive reports about the land flowing with milk and honey. They are willing to endure additional years of wilderness wandering because the anxiety attached to a new beginning feels intolerable.

Bridges teaches that true beginnings follow the timing of spirit, mind, and heart. A new start is not synonymous with a new beginning. The new start happens in response to an event—the building is opened, the new pastor arrives, the new worship service begins. A new beginning happens when the people are spiritually and emotionally ready to move out of liminality and into a new chapter of life.

New beginnings continue to feel frightening to people for many reasons. The leader of a community emerging from liminality can expect these reactions:[22]

- Old anxieties that were originally triggered at the time of separation begin to reemerge. People will feel that they are still experiencing losses of one kind or another.
- The new way represents a gamble, which makes people fearful. We still don't know a proven way, and there is always the possibility that our approach won't work.
- The uncertainty of the new way reminds people of old failures; it may trigger institutional memory of trauma or failure.
- Liminality had its own appeal and people may wish to linger there. Perhaps some people felt less marginalized in a season of liminality and they fear being excluded once again, now that a new normal is emerging. Some may have enjoyed the freedom of experimentation and living with less accountability. They don't particularly value the structures and procedures that will accompany reorientation. Finally, some will question their ability to learn new ways. Fear of personal failure may keep them in a permanently liminal space.

I recently interviewed a pastor who was retiring after twenty-seven years of faithful and effective leadership in the same congregation. His high-profile ministry was marked by many personal and congregational leadership triumphs. He was preparing to hand over the reins of a vibrant and growing ministry. Here is the essence of what he shared with me about his own beginnings as a leader.

> I have had many successful years of ministry here, but the beginning was not easy. I followed another pastor who led the congregation for eighteen powerful years prior to my arrival. It didn't appear at first that the congregation was going to accept my leadership. In fact, it was six full years before they granted me the authority to lead. It wasn't six years of misery. We had some successes. But it was clearly six years before they began to trust me to drive the thing.

Heifetz and Linsky describe many leadership challenges during a season of reorientation. One is the need to let the people do their own adaptive work. A leader cannot impose reorientation on a people not yet ready to yield. Solutions are achieved when "the people with the problem" go through a process together to become "the people with the solution."[23] This requires more than changed minds—it requires changed hearts and behavior.

The work of the leader then is as much about presence as it is about action. The leader provides interpretations and gives meaning to what the people are encountering, designs effective interventions that help people learn, acts politically to expand his influence base, protects and engages the voices of dissent, and orchestrates conflict to continue the hard work of adaptation.[24] You can read more about this kind of leadership activity in chapter 7.

A DIFFERENT WAY OF LEADING

A liminal season requires a personal presence that is different from leadership during stable times. Problematically, however, many church leaders invest their energy in traditional leadership activities: vision casting, advocating for big new ideas, striving for growth, and mastering new skills. These practices may provide a false sense of control and momentum; however, they don't fundamentally impact liminality.

An effective leader must help individuals and groups remain in a liminal state for the time that it takes to get clear about identity and to discover new structures that are more appropriately suited to their emerging identity. They must invite and work with communitas. Leading in a liminal season requires helping people manage their anxiety, embrace the freedom of unknowing, explore new possible identities and pathways, and resist the temptation to reorient people before they are ready.

In traditional seasons of stability, leaders are selected and rewarded for their ability to restore order and reinforce the status quo. Traditional leadership focuses on striving to produce new outcomes and to advance mission. These are the activities that we typically honor when we recognize outstanding leadership. In liminal seasons, traditional leadership activities are exhausting and unproductive.

Leadership in a liminal season rarely looks outstanding to the random observer. In fact, leading effectively in a liminal season is incredibly dangerous work because people are generally not happy with the individual who guides them through the hard work of loss, grief, and letting go. People often want to reject leaders that are doing effective liminal work because those leaders are making them feel uncomfortable.

It is much easier to be the kind of leader that strives to restore what was, the leader who makes people feel safe and happy. But that leader rarely takes the organization any place meaningful in a liminal era. That kind of leader often drags an organization back into its preliminal state, so that no adaptation takes place.

Moses' leadership presence during the wilderness wandering was not remarkable for the mileage covered, the growth of the community under his leadership, or the productivity of the community. Moses' leadership during liminality is remarkable because of the new national identity that he birthed, following God's lead.

Moses does not enter the promised land with the people. His part of the biblical story only involved liminal season leadership. Moses emerges at the end of an era; he watches over the disintegration of the social structure that oppressed his people in slavery. Moses guides them through their liminal era and then turns the leadership reins over to the next generation. There is little in the way of accountable success in Moses' story, and yet he is one of our greatest leadership heroes.

Most of us will not be in leadership on the other side of this liminal era. The individual congregations we lead may move in and out of seasons of liminality, but the institutional Church will likely remain liminal for some time. Like Moses, we may never enter the promised land. We are liminal leaders, charged with taking the Church through this scary season of disorientation, disengagement, and disenchantment.

We can choose to throw our hands up in despair, but that will not be helpful to our constituents or the institution. We can choose to set audacious goals, cast bold new visions, and wrestle our way toward a new beginning. That approach may provide a false sense of propulsion. It will not impact liminality.

Instead, we can approach this era with a different leadership stance, engaging a different body of leadership work. We can let go of our egoic need to look successful and lead instead from a place of open wonder and curiosity. We can be led by the future itself as we discover the mind of Christ for the heart of the Church.

The remainder of this book will guide you through the components of effective leadership in a liminal season. We will explore a different kind of leadership presence (chapter 2). Then you will be introduced to the soul of the institution as the guiding force for discerning a pathway forward (chapter 3). The final four chapters of the book will introduce you to four valuable bodies of work worth pursuing in a liminal season. You will learn how to deepen group discernment practices (chapter 4), shape institutional memory (chapter 5), clarify purpose (chapter 6), and engage emergence (chapter 7).

The work of a leader in a liminal season is not easy, and it is almost never pretty. However, it may be the most important and ultimately rewarding thing that you do in your lifetime. Let's get started.

NOTES

1. Richard Rohr, *Everything Belongs: The Gift of Contemplative Prayer* (New York: The Crossroad Publishing Company, 1999), 155–56.

2. Charles La Shure, "What Is Liminality?" *Histories and Theories of Intermedia*, October 18, 2005. http://umintermediai501.blogspot.com/2008/12/what-is-liminality-charles-la-shure.html. Accessed June 29, 2018.

3. Arpad Szakolczai, "Liminality and Experience: Structuring Transitory Situations and Transformative Events," *International Political Anthropology Journal 2*, no. 1 (2009): 152.

4. La Shure, "What Is Liminality?"

5. Bjorn Thomassen, "Liminality," in *The Encyclopedia of Social Theory*, edited by Austin Harrington, Barbara L. Marshall, and Hans-Peter Müller (London, UK: Psychology Press, 2006), 322.

6. Victor Turner, "Betwixt and Between: The Liminal Period in Rites de Passage," in *The Forest of Symbols* (Ithaca, NY: Cornell University Press, 1967), 97.

7. Szakolczai, "Liminality and Experience," 151.

8. Phyllis Tickle, *The Great Emergence: How Christianity Is Changing and Why* (Grand Rapids, MI: Baker Books, 2008), 19–32.

9. Michelle Boorsteing, "Acts of Faith," *The Washington Post*, April 6, 2016.

10. Diana Butler Bass, *Grounded: Finding God in the World—A Spiritual Revolution* (New York: Harper Collins Publishing, 2015).

11. Bjorn Thomassen, "The Uses and Meanings of Liminality," *International Political Anthropology Journal 2*, no. 1 (2009): 18.

12. William Bridges, *Managing Transitions: Making the Most of Change* (third edition) (Philadelphia, PA: DeCapo Press, 2009), 4.

13. Ronald Heifetz, Alexander Grashow, and Marty Linsky, *The Practice of Adaptive Leadership: Tools and Tactics for Changing Your Organization and the World* (Boston, MA: Harvard Business Press, 2009), 22–23.

14. Bridges, *Managing Transitions*, 34.

15. Bridges, *Managing Transitions*, 34–36.

16. Bridges, *Managing Transitions*, 37–47.

17. Ronald A. Heifetz and Marty Linsky, *Leadership on the Line: Staying Alive through the Dangers of Leading* (Boston, MA: Harvard Business Press, 2002), 9–18.

18. These approaches to raising and lowering the temperature of the congregation are adapted from Heifetz, Linsky, and Grashow, *The Practice of Adaptive Leadership*, 160.

19. Victor Turner, "Liminality and Communitas," in *The Ritual Process: Structure and Anti-Structure* (New York: Routledge Press, 2017), 95–96.

20. John Philip Newell, *Celtic Prayers from Iona* (New York: Paulist Press, 1997), 7.

21. Szakolczai, "Liminality and Experience," 154.

22. Bridges, *Managing Transitions*, 50–52.

23. Heifetz and Linsky, *Leadership on the Line*, 123–39.

24. Heifetz, Grashow, and Linsky, *The Practice of Adaptive Leadership*, 109–11.

Chapter Two

Leading with Presence

Holding Steady

Thus am I, a feather on the breath of God.
—Hildegaard of Bingen

The authenticity of any leadership action depends upon the interior condition of the leader—on his or her ability to be true to self and true to the institution, to remain non-anxious, and to connect with the Divine.

When the interior condition of the leader is rooted in personal ego, the attention of the leader is inauthentic, not attuned to the needs of the organization. Instead, the ego creates an image of the leader that the self will admire, and that will garner the admiration of others.

Consider this example. Miranda wants to do what is right for her congregation. But equally important, Miranda wants to be admired as the youngest and first female pastor appointed to lead this congregation. She is striving to demonstrate mastery of complex leadership demands. She wants others to admire her leadership. She needs the church to grow under her watch. Miranda has been captured by her ego self and will have a hard time discerning what God is calling forth from her or from the congregation. Unless she can relinquish these ego-driven expectations, Miranda will have little hope of leading this congregation authentically.

Authentic leadership is especially critical in liminal seasons. As we explored in chapter 1, liminal seasons elicit disorientation and dysfunction. They also invite creativity and imagination. To negotiate the dysfunction and tap into the creativity, an authority figure must lead as an authentic self, a self fully rooted in the Divine and free from the false constructs of the ego. The true self leads from a place of wonder, with suspended expectations about what ought to happen next.

Throughout this book, the term Presence will be used to define a leadership stance born of the authentic self, unencumbered by ego, and led by the Divine. One who is leading with Presence is free to explore the questions: Who am I? What is being called forth from this organization? How, then, shall I lead?

Presence has its roots in the Christian wisdom tradition of Contemplation. Contemplation is an ongoing discipline of seeing events, people, and issues through the lens of "God Consciousness." We practice letting go of personal agendas, our own anger, fear, and judgments. In the empty space created by this release, we invite God to speak and we seek to listen. With contemplative hearts, we live openly and lead with mercy and patience. We embrace our own vulnerability and become generous toward the unsettling issues facing us in the here and now.[1]

Presence, then, is a leadership awareness characterized by an openness to wonder. Presence demonstrates a willingness to experiment, take risks, and learn from mistakes. It is guided by Spirit, and it is willing to face failure. Presence is knowing that emerges from the intelligence of the heart and spirit—from a place of wisdom. In a state of Presence, we recognize our God-given self, interdependent with the God-given self of the institution we lead.

WHAT PRESENCE LOOKS LIKE

Stonecrest Community Church is known as the place to go if you are looking for excellence in traditional worship. A Sunday morning attendee can expect a biblically based and compelling thirty-minute sermon, organ music played on the finest pipe organ within a twenty-mile radius, and a one hundred voice classical choir, accompanied by stringed instruments. Sunday mornings at Stonecrest are an event.

Stonecrest Community has been at its present location for fifteen years, a church replant born from a one-time foundering congregation, one that was so diminished it was ready to close its doors. In the fifteen years since relocating, the congregation has grown to twelve hundred in weekly worship attendance. A much-loved pastor, who guided the move and oversaw the tremendous growth of the congregation, retired three years ago. One of the final things that he said to the congregation was that they should never abandon their roots as a church worshiping in the traditional style.

In the hype that surrounded relocation, new buildings, paying off mortgages, and their pastor's retirement, no one payed much attention to the fact that worship attendance had begun to decline. Two years ago, the congregation called Pastor Marcus as their new senior leader. Marcus was well-received by the congregation, but he is young and still earning his leadership stripes. The pastoral transition did not lead to automatic growth in worship attendance, as some had hoped, and now leaders are paying close attention. They are beginning to worry and wonder, "What should we do about worship attendance? Who, or what, is responsible for our decline?"

Pastor Marcus has good reason to be anxious about the worship conversations unfolding in the congregation. Anxiety is on the rise. Many are convicted by the strong departing words of the previous pastor, "The best way forward is to honor the legacy of our past—traditional worship." This group advocates putting resources into what they've always done well. Simultaneously, there are those threatening to leave the church if the congregation doesn't introduce more contemporary worship; worship experiences that welcome informality, involve praise music and percussive instruments, and invite an emotive response.

Marcus fears that the future of his ministry lies in the balance. People are watching to see how he negotiates this question. No one has directly challenged his leadership yet, but Marcus knows that people are wondering why his preaching and youthful presence haven't brought more people into worship. Marcus worries that he is to blame for the congregation's failure to thrive.

On his worst days Marcus is captured by his own anxiety and the anxiety of the congregation. He becomes fearful about his own future in ministry. He gathers like-minded leaders around him, and they do their best to marginalize the voices of the "trouble makers." Marcus reads literature about worship trends and silently prepares a case for sustaining the traditional worship trajectory of the congregation, the style of worship that he feels most comfortable leading. He consults with other pastoral leaders about how to quell an anxious congregation in times like this one.

On his best days, however, Marcus is a different kind of leader. He leads with Presence. He incorporates a regular practice of seeking stillness, so that his leadership choices originate from a centered place. He detaches himself from any one outcome about the future of worship at Stonecrest Community Church. He listens deeply. He inwardly acknowledges that what is best for the future of the church might involve his departure. Marcus realizes that he will likely be made the scapegoat for any bad decisions made. He moves the conversation forward anyway.

Marcus listens thoughtfully to the voices of those who oppose the status quo. He leads the congregation through a six-week sermon series on worship, so that all share a common language for dialogue. He assembles a group of spiritually mature leaders to begin a study/listening process. They pray. They host a series of dialogue circles to listen to the voice of the congregation and the longings of its spirit. Marcus confronts those congregants who behave badly when their anxiety gets the worst of them, always inviting his leaders back to a spiritual stance of wonder. When congregants vent their frustration at Marcus, he regulates his personal emotional reactions, so that those reactions don't color his leadership choices.

On his best days, Marcus embraces the unknown for all that it might teach him. He surrenders to the hard work and the possibility of failure. He isn't perfect. The congregation isn't perfect. They all make mistakes along the way, and they sometimes become reactive. However, as they lead with Presence, they discern a pathway forward for Stonecrest Community Church.

We will hear more about their process and their group discernment in chapter 4 of this book. For purposes of this chapter, we are most interested in Marcus' leadership stance. What equips Marcus to lead with Presence in the face of mounting anxiety?

PRESENCE: A QUALITY OF AWARENESS

Every outward leadership action originates from an inner source—the consciousness of the one who is leading. Consciousness is the quality of awareness that we bring to bear on a situation. Our consciousness impacts the actions we take and the decisions we make. When leading, most of us are aware of *what* we do and what others do. We are also aware of *how* we do things, the processes that we follow when we act. Most of us are less aware of *why* we do what we do, the inner source from which our actions arise.[2]

Viktor Frankl, an Austrian psychiatrist and survivor of the Holocaust, is often credited with this famous quote, "Between stimulus and response, there is a space. In that space is our power to choose our response. In our response lies our growth and our freedom."[3] The space between stimulus and response, the space that allows us to interpret and choose, this is our consciousness.

Consciousness is formed by our past experiences and our psychological profile. For example, when I open the fridge at home and see it packed with lots of fresh produce, I celebrate abundance. I anticipate with delight all the possible meals that I might concoct from those precious fruits and vegetables. When my husband opens the same fridge, he is filled with an overwhelming sense of responsibility for eating all those fruits and veggies before they go bad. He wonders why I would take the risk of purchasing so much produce all at one time. Each of us interprets the same reality (a well-stocked fridge) differently. My consciousness about food is shaped by a family that celebrated life through food. His family taught him to be a careful steward of food as a precious and limited resource. My husband and I make remarkably different purchasing decisions at the grocery store given our consciousness about food.

Consider this organizational example. A pastor and a board leader meet for a conversation about an upcoming stewardship campaign. The pastor is a young woman whose only leadership experience is in the church. She is small of stature and has been manipulated and intimidated by male leaders in the past. The board leader is a burly middle-aged man who successfully leads a local non-profit. The board leader attempts to offer some friendly advice about fundraising, drawn from his many years of leadership experience. In their exchange, the pastor believes that she is being bullied by a member of the congregation who doesn't have a clue about what it takes to run a congregation. The board leader believes that he has been disrespected and that his heartfelt and sound advice has been rudely ignored.

Each leader enters the exchange with a consciousness that is not apparent to the other. This causes confusion, and biases are reinforced in the ensuing conversation. The exchange is non-productive, and both leaders feel unheard, offended, and underappreciated. Sound familiar? Let's figure out what happened.

RESTRICTED AWARENESS

Otto Scharmer, senior lecturer at the Massachusetts Institute of Technology and founder of the Presencing Institute, refers to the leader's consciousness as a "field of attention." The field of our attention is formed by learned patterns of the past. We pay attention to the reality in front of us through habitual judgments. Scharmer uses the term "downloading" to describe our habitual mode of interpreting the present reality in light of past experience.[4]

When we download, our learning is limited to reconfirming what we already know to be true. "I know this lay leader is going to bully me into accepting his personal agenda." Nothing new permeates our bubble of interpretation. We only hear what we have already determined to be true.

When we download, we make sense of the whole organization by placing self at the center. We may refer to this mental activity as thinking, but it is more aptly known as downloading, because it is unexamined and reactive. Consider the diagram on the following page, in which the dot represents you at the center of your perceived universe. You see the organization that you serve as a closed system, a universe defined by you that is fully understandable by you and known only by you.

When downloading, we are unaware of all that informs our situation. We operate with blind spots. Our blind spots are formed by the assumptions we make without realizing that we are assuming.

Spiritual director and author Tilden Edwards points out the important role of language and story in the formation of our blind spots. The power and the familiarity of our own words can blind us to interpretations we have made.

Downloading

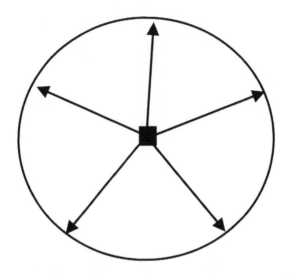

We see things as "really real" simply because of the story we tell about our recalled experience.[5] We convince ourselves that our reflection on our experience is the same as the experience itself, that it captures the fullness of all that may have happened.

Let's revisit the scenario between the pastor and the board leader. Neither party can see beyond their blind spots—the assumptions they have made about who they are and what the other is trying to do.

The pastor sees herself as a victim of male intimidation. The facts surrounding any previous bullying experience are irrelevant. What matters is that she has interpreted her prior exchanges with male leaders as threatening and has learned to frame her story through the lens of victimization. Furthermore, the pastor desperately wants to be regarded as a capable organizational leader. In the past, some have questioned her organizational abilities. When the board leader approaches her with some "friendly advice," she believes that he is bullying her and critiquing her skills. She is operating from her blind spot.

The board leader sees himself as a magnanimous colleague offering sound advice to a less experienced mentee. He considers stories of his past success at fundraising and mentoring. However, he also wants to be regarded as a generous soul. In the past, some have accused him of being self-serving.

When the pastor shuns his well-meaning advice, it triggers those previous critiques and his generosity is once again at stake. He is held captive by his blind spot.

We will explore ways to release our blind spots later in the chapter. For now, let's seek to understand what an expanded awareness—free of blind spots—looks like.

EXPANDING AWARENESS

Scharmer says that we achieve fuller consciousness when we learn to expand our field of attention—when we learn to view the organization from the periphery, sensing the greater whole—when we learn to view our situation from an emerging future, rather than from our limiting past.

The diagram on the following page illustrates an expansive field of attention. We stop viewing the organization as a closed system that we negotiate from the center. We see things from a broader vantage point, one that allows us to gain fresh perspective, incorporating a more comprehensive understanding of the environment, the players, and their motivations. We invite things into the boundary of our experience that were previously excluded.

Revisiting our case study, the pastor shifts her field of attention when she chooses to overlook the delivery style of the message from the board leader and attends instead to the information being shared. She chooses not to be offended. Simultaneously, the board leader shifts his field of attention by listening to the pastor's feedback, recognizing that his communication style is getting in the way of his message.

The board leader begins the next conversation by asking the pastor's opinion first, about how the circumstances of congregational life might demand something other than what has been successful in his non-profit. Their dialogue leads to the development of an innovative stewardship campaign. Both the pastor and the board leader are honored in the exchange.

Management consultants Heifetz and Linsky describe this shift in consciousness as "getting on the balcony above the dance floor."[6] Truly understanding the organization requires distance from the events happening directly in front of you. If you only stay on the dance floor, all you will see is the people dancing around you. You can get swept up in the party and carried away by the music, but you can't assess or influence the larger dance. When you get up on the balcony you see a different picture. You notice that certain people aren't dancing at all, that others are hanging near the exits and are ready to bolt, that a musician has a broken instrument, that the party isn't so great after all. If someone asks you to describe the party later, you will describe it very differently depending on whether you were on the dance floor or on the balcony. An effective leader moves continuously between the

Expanded Awareness

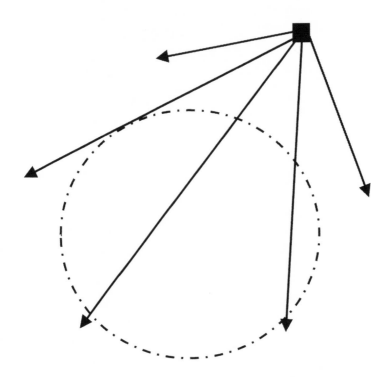

dance floor and the balcony to develop an expanded awareness of the organ-ization, while influencing what is happening on the dance floor.

In a liminal season we must teach the leaders that we serve to see and sense themselves differently, to challenge their field of awareness and to discover their blind spots. We cannot invite others to this work if we our-selves operate with limited awareness.

PUTTING ON CHRIST CONSCIOUSNESS

Christians often speak about putting on the mind of Christ. Scriptures in the Christian tradition speak of Christ consciousness. "And it is no longer I who live, but it is Christ who lives in me" (Galatians 2:20). "Let the same mind be in you that was in Christ Jesus" (Philippians 2:5).

We see things more fully and attend to our environment more authentically when we open ourselves to Christ consciousness. This is the essence of becoming our true selves. "We lose ourselves in order to find ourselves" (Mark 8:35).

The great contemplatives throughout the ages have taught about dying and letting go, about finding peace and contentment through shedding and letting come. Thomas Merton, the Cistercian monk, introduced the term "false self" to describe the ego self that captures us when we are not letting go, not fully centered in God.[7]

The false self is an illusion, our egoic self. It is an identity of our own creation, heavily influenced by societal and cultural norms, overly invested in impressing others, demonstrating superiority over others, and maintaining control. The false self emerges when we are overly reliant on ourselves, and when we are outside of relationship with the Divine. Merton describes it this way:

> Every one of us is shadowed by an illusory person: a false self. This is the man that I want myself to be but who cannot exist, because God does not know anything about him. And to be unknown of God is altogether too much privacy. . . . A life devoted to the cult of this shadow figure is what is called a life of sin. . . .
>
> All sin starts from the assumption that my false self, the self that exists only in my own egocentric desires, is the fundamental reality of life to which everything else in the universe is ordered. Thus, I use up my life in the desire for pleasures and the thirst for experiences, for power, honor, knowledge and love, to clothe this false self and construct its nothingness into something objectively real.[8]

The true self is the self that is known and loved by God, nothing more and nothing less. Merton uses a variety of images to describe the essence of the true self.

> The true self is like: a mirror in which God sees the divine self; a little world illumined by the light of Christ; an inexhaustible resource for self-sacrificing love; a special place where God's name is written; a point of pure truth at the center of our being; a temple where God dwells; a center point or apex of the soul responsive to the Holy Spirit.[9]

The true self is the authentic free self that is in full relationship with God and fully capable of love—for self, for others, and for the world. It is the divine indwelling of God within me, and me within God.

Pastor Lindsay was born to preach; at least this is how she understands her call into ministry. From a young age Lindsay distinguished herself as a masterful storyteller. She excelled at using language, particularly in public speaking contexts, where she delighted others with her storytelling, and she grew to impress others with her skills as teacher, persuader, and influencer. Lindsay was ordained and became the solo pastor of a small congregation ten years ago. She and her congregation thrived together. Many in the surrounding area began to hear of her preaching skill. Eventually she captured the attention of a much larger congregation three towns over, one that was looking for a new senior minister. Lindsay accepted the new call and eagerly began a new chapter in her vocational life.

Things went well for the first eighteen months. She was a fresh voice in a pulpit that had long been known for heady, intellectual preaching. The committee that nominated Lindsay told her that she was just what they had been looking for, an alternative to the dry, expository preaching they had all grown weary of. Lindsay was thrilled to step into this larger preaching arena and was eager to lead a multi-staff team.

Somewhere around the eighteen-month mark, the tide began to turn on Lindsay's popularity. A small but vocal constituency in the congregation began grumbling that Lindsay wasn't intellectual enough to sustain this pulpit or to stimulate this congregation. Her training wasn't prestigious enough, her stories were silly, and she spent too much time talking to them about Jesus in a homespun sappy way that they were beginning to resent. They wanted more intellectual stimulation from the pulpit, and they didn't think Lindsay was up to the task.

The troublemakers elevated their complaining and infected others with their anxious grumbling. Members of the personnel committee met with Lindsay to talk about the complaints they were hearing. Lindsay's own anxiety escalated. She had begun to mistrust herself in this pulpit, so she agreed to experiment with different preaching styles.

Lindsay increased the time she spent on sermon preparation and began to neglect her other duties as head of staff. She changed the types of literature she was reading. She listened to the sermons of her predecessor and tried to mirror his style. Within six months, Lindsay played into the grumblers' worst expectations of her. Her preaching style became inauthentic, dry, unimaginative, and uninspiring. Her efforts at appearing more intellectual backfired, and instead she appeared to be drowning. She made serious mistakes in other parts of her role as well. Lindsay was clearly failing in her new assignment.

What happened to Lindsay is a universal experience. We lose sight of our authentic selves and begin chasing an ego persona, an image that we or someone else imposes upon us as an ideal. Then we measure our worthiness by our success at chasing the false ideal.

Lindsay's true self, a beloved child of God, has a remarkable preaching gift. Her gift may or may not be right for this congregation. But when Lindsay lost sight of her own inherent worthiness and giftedness, she abandoned any possibility of satisfying herself, God, or this congregation. She embraced a false self. It was the false self that failed.

The false self lacks Presence. The false self will always be reactive, anxious, and striving. The false self has a narrow field of attention. The false self restricts the boundaries of its own awareness, because it is invested in self-protection and self-promotion. The false self cannot bolster leadership in a liminal season, when so much is in turmoil. The false self cannot invite a better quality of awareness.

When Lindsay began to fail in the pulpit, she encountered an existential crisis. "If I am not an outstanding preacher, then who am I?" She began to imagine that she had lost favor with God and that she had lost her vocation and calling. Gradually, through work with a spiritual director and a leadership coach, Lindsay developed a practice of spiritual discipline and began to regain her leadership footing. In time she rediscovered her authentic preaching voice. With the support of helpful lay leaders, she rode out the criticism of the grumblers who didn't value her style. A small group of ten left the church once they realized that Lindsay wasn't going anywhere. Lindsay survived this leadership crisis and emerged on the other side of the experience with greater influence in her congregation. She began to lead with Presence, from her authentic God-centered self—and the congregation felt the difference.

ILLUMINATING OUR BLIND SPOTS

The false self and blind spots go hand in hand. It is hard to say which comes first, as they reinforce one another. We develop blind spots, and in our blindness, we develop a false self. Our false self feeds on the darkness of the blind spots. Otto Scharmer says that a leader with Presence is aware of his or her own blind spots and illumines those blind spots to be able to lead with:

- Open Mind: The capacity to suspend habitual judgment.
- Open Heart: The capacity to shift perspective from my viewpoint to the viewpoint of others.
- Open Will: The capacity to let go of preconceived outcomes and let come what wants to emerge from the future. [10]

Leaders unaware of their blind spots demonstrate pathologies in their leadership choices. Unaware leaders are tempted to believe that they have only one self, that there is only one way to view their situation, and that there is only one truth to be honored in the choices that need to be made. Such leaders function with a closed mind, closed heart, and closed will. This leader is trapped by the past, unable to function well in the present, and incapable of leading toward an emerging future.

Consider this example. Cityscape is a food program for the working poor
and homeless that operates on the campus of Eatonville Church. The congregation birthed the ministry ten years ago as one of several social justice
programs. Over time, the needs of the ministry outgrew the capacity of the
church. Today, Cityscape manages an operating budget that is larger than the
operating budget of the church. Cityscape operates as an independent
501(c)(3) but maintains strong ties to the congregation. It is still housed on
church grounds and pays no rent to the congregation. Many church leaders
serve on the board of the non-profit, and congregants heavily support the
ministry, both financially and with volunteer hours.

Today, however, the relationship between the Cityscape board and the
congregation's board is tense. The church board spends up to 60 percent of
its time and energy trying to resolve conflicts between Cityscape and the
congregation. Church board leaders feel that Cityscape places too many demands on the congregation, such as asking that the weekend education
classes held in the Cityscape wing of the building be relocated elsewhere.
Board Chairperson Conrad and Cityscape's executive director, Debbie, also
have a very troubled relationship, due in part to their different political and
theological perspectives.

Conrad is stuck. He doesn't know how to lead in this situation. He has
many understandable blind spots. His ego is invested in retaining church
ownership of this large and vibrant ministry. He doesn't want Cityscape to go
elsewhere and give some other congregation credit for his congregation's
good work. He is fearful of the reaction of congregants if Cityscape leaves.

At the same time, Conrad desperately wants to reassign the building space
that Cityscape occupies to a much-needed youth house. He wants relief from
the demands of this pesky tenant. Conrad has heard that Debbie gossips
about Conrad's leadership ability with congregants who volunteer at Cityscape. Conrad wants to be free of Debbie.

Conrad sees only two possible choices on the horizon. Throw Cityscape
out, or let it continue to run roughshod over the needs of the congregation.
Conrad is operating with a closed mind, closed heart, and closed will. Conse-
quently, he has been unable to resolve these recurring complaints, which
have been dragging on for years.

Otto Scharmer suggests that one of the ways we illuminate, and eventually release, our blind spots is by attending to three internal voices that limit us.
These are the voices of judgment, cynicism, and fear. These voices dominate
the thinking of a leader with blind spots.[11]

The Voice of Judgment

The voice of judgment is certain about many things. It creates black/white,
either/or choices. It is the voice in your head that makes meaning out of your

present circumstance based on past fears. It reduces the complexity of any situation by creating simple, concrete interpretations about events.

The voice of judgment shuts down the open mind. The voice of judgment keeps interpretations easy, negatively labeling issues that are threatening or don't seem to belong. Let's listen to the voice of judgment as it operates inside of Conrad's head.

> It is no longer in our best interest to house this ministry. We are financing their growth as a non-profit at the expense of our church operating budget. People mistakenly believe that giving to Cityscape supports the church, because they don't understand the legal distinction between the two entities. Cityscape has become too demanding in their usage of our building, and their needs are likely to keep escalating. Discipleship in the congregation is suffering at the hands of social justice ministry. If we don't meet all their demands, Cityscape will leave us and find space elsewhere.

Notice the all-or-nothing thinking and the stark conclusions that are drawn by the voice of judgment. Much of what the voice says is accurate, but it spins the story in such a way that there is little hope of finding a solution. Quieting this voice requires self-reflection and distinguishing between what is real and what is imagined. If Conrad wants to eliminate his blind spots, he needs to adopt a stance of wonder about his starkly drawn conclusions, those judgments created by his all or nothing mindset. Only then will he be able to identify other possibilities. Only then can he discover a hopeful future waiting to emerge.

The Voice of Cynicism

Cynicism is the second voice identified by Scharmer. The voice of cynicism is sharp, snarky, and inclined to believe that others are only motivated by personal self-interest. Cynicism is the voice in the leader's head that is skeptical, doubtful, mistrusting, suspicious, and disbelieving. It shuts down the pathway to an open heart. Its purpose is to protect the leader from an emotional investment in ideas that could damage the ego. Listen for the voice of cynicism in this version of Conrad's experience:

> It is easy for the Cityscape ministry to appear so successful when they don't have to finance any of their own overhead. Cityscape board leaders are only interested in getting as much as they can from the church. They don't care about any of the rest of our ministries. The executive director is out to make me look bad as a leader. She is the worst example of liberal minded social consciousness run amok. If we don't put our foot down against their demands soon, they will take us over. This is a case of the tail wagging the dog. There isn't any way to negotiate a better relationship with Cityscape, because they will just slip into their old demanding behavior time after time.

Notice how the voice of cynicism likes to attach pejorative labels. This voice does not want Conrad to be vulnerable or tender-hearted. It does not give his opponent any benefit of the doubt. The voice of cynicism is invested in creating winners and losers and wants to make sure that Conrad remains on the winning side. This voice is masterful at dismissing opposing viewpoints by belittling the intentions of the one with a different point of view.

To expand his awareness, Conrad needs to challenge the voice of cynicism. He needs to invite a more whole-hearted, open stance. He needs to cultivate his capacity for vulnerability, his willingness to suffer at the hands of another if that should come to pass. Only then will he be able to call forth the best from those that he leads. Only then will his thinking become more generative, hope-filled, and loving. Only then will he rediscover his true self.

The Voice of Fear

The voice of fear is the final of the three voices that contribute to a leader's blind spots. The voice of fear does not want you to consider options, because options might get you into trouble. This is the voice in your head that plays upon your worst imagining, by scaring you with negative scenarios. The voice of fear wants you to believe that your world is not safe and that your leadership status is in danger. Fear wants you to believe in the worst possible outcome. The voice of fear shuts down the open will. It wants you to pursue the status quo as a safety net, and it likes to remind you of all the ways in which your self-interests will be damaged by surrendering to the unknown. Let's listen in to the voice of fear in Conrad's head:

> If Cityscape leaves the building, we will not survive the fallout. Members of the congregation will turn against me and the pastor. The executive director will use her relationships in the congregation to build her support base, and she will take the congregants that support Cityscape to whatever new church home she finds for the ministry. I might as well pack my bags and look for my next church, if we decide that Cityscape must go.

To suspend the voice of fear, Conrad must learn to recognize opportunity in failure. Releasing the voice of fear requires releasing a desire for control. Conrad must be willing to acknowledge that he cannot control all the variables that determine the next outcome. Yielding to whatever might occur, the fully conscious leader considers the known options and chooses a course of action with open mind, open heart, and open will. Whatever happens after the choice is made will present further opportunities for growth and reflection. There is nothing to fear because every possible outcome is grounded in the goodness of God's indwelling Spirit.

In the end, through the discipline of prayer and personal reflection, Conrad was able to set aside the voices of judgment, cynicism, and fear. Then, he was able to engage Debbie in imagining several options that had not been evident when he was locked in dialogue with the three voices. Ultimately, the two boards crafted a lease with Cityscape that required the payment of rent in exchange for more dedicated space. Conrad and Debbie discovered a win/win scenario that had not been possible earlier when both leaders were operating with closed mind, heart, and will.

THREE SPIRITUAL SHIFTS

We have been exploring various ways of inviting Presence into a leader's stance. So far, we have explored how to use self-awareness to expand consciousness. Now we are going to focus on three spiritual shifts that invite Presence. The three shifts include moving from knowing to unknowing, from advocating to attending, and from striving to surrendering.

None of these shifts are encouraged by our culture, because this work entails vulnerability. Our culture values leaders who know many things and promote what they know. Our culture values leaders who have strong viewpoints about how to proceed and who staunchly advocate those viewpoints. Our culture values leaders who strive to overcome any obstacles that stand in the way of success. To do otherwise is to open ourselves to accusations of weakness. Nevertheless, leading with Presence requires this vulnerability.

From Knowing to Unknowing

The shift from knowing to unknowing begins with a decision to become suspicious of our own thinking. We acknowledge that our thinking minds are captured by our ego. The shift from knowing to unknowing is an interior act of suspension. We slow down our thinking, observe our judgments, and recognize our own compulsions and ego-centric concerns. We examine the assumptions that shape our conclusions. We recognize that we are not our thoughts, and that we have the capacity to observe and suspend our thoughts in service to a better way of seeing.

We don't have to be limited by our own knowledge. Rather, we can tap into spiritual intuition—a direct knowing from God. This awareness is activated when we are willing to observe thoughts that pass through our mind without being owned by those thoughts. We move toward unknowing when we rest in the openness that appears between our thoughts. [12]

Traditional practices of leadership expect a leader to apply the best of what they know to an identified problem or challenge. By contrast, leading with Presence invites us to unknow, to drop preconceived certainties about how things ought to unfold, to acknowledge that God's work within an organization is mysterious.

This is frightening work for the leader, pastor, or professor who has been authorized to lead by virtue of demonstrated expertise. We are given permission to lead because people trust that we know things, and they trust our ability to apply our knowledge to solve organizational problems. If we fail to deliver people from their problems, they may turn on us.

I discovered this incapacitating vulnerability when I first began my studies in spiritual direction. As I studied, I encountered a recurring theme in the literature of the contemplative tradition. To seek communion with God, we must relinquish our need for control and our certainty about what we know. We must yield to uncertainty. I began to embrace these practices in my personal life in the first year of the program, but I kept that discipline separate from my professional life.

By the second year of the program I began to discern a new vocational calling. Others in the program were planning to take the practice of spiritual direction into one-on-one helping relationships with others. I, on the other hand, was feeling called to bring the disciplines of contemplation and the practice of spiritual direction into my consulting practice, into the life of organizations. I felt called to serve as a spiritual director to institutions.

Once this calling emerged with clarity, I experienced a professional crisis. I knew that I needed to incorporate a contemplative stance in the daily practice of my work. This amounted to much more than having a centering prayer time at the beginning of each day.

In the daily engagement of my work I needed to practice unknowing. But here is the rub: People pay a consultant to know many things, to bring outside expertise into the organization. How could I embrace an unknowing stance and still make a living? Could I protect my brand as an "expert" in the leadership of large congregations and still embrace an unknowing stance? Wouldn't leading with Presence cast me as a weak consultant in the eyes of my constituents?

I struggled with this dilemma for at least two years. In all honesty, I still regularly succumb to a temptation to flaunt the little expertise that I have. But I have learned a thing or two along the way, lessons that have helped me own an unknowing stance more consistently.

First, I realized that unknowing is not the same thing as ignorance. To adopt an unknowing stance, I do not need to abandon knowledge. I continue to learn many factual things that serve my clients well. However, I have learned to view my own knowledge with suspicion. I am learning when to set it aside in service to being led into the unknown. If I am overly reliant on all that I know, I am not open to Presence and the mystery of my faith, the need for awe, the beauty in wisdom.

Second, people respect a leader who offers knowledge without holding tightly to what is known. People respect a leader who has the courage to acknowledge when a challenge deserves more than an easy platitude or a pretend solution. People respect the leader who says, "I really don't know the answer, but I'm willing to stand here with you in the anxiety of our mutual not knowing."

Finally, I have learned that when I get too full of my own knowing, God is always at the ready to right-size my ego. Recently, I facilitated a leadership retreat for a congregation engaged in strategic planning. We had eight hours of scheduled time to complete a significant body of work. I assembled a carefully detailed plan for how the event would unfold. It is a design I have used in many other contexts, and I know that the process works when we stay on track. We must follow the plan to get the work done. Keeping people on track is one of my best skills.

I arrived at the facility an hour before the retreat began, along with the other planning leaders. We spent some time in prayer, and then we busied ourselves with the setup of the room. Thirty minutes before we were scheduled to begin, Joel arrived. I had not met Joel in any of my previous work at the church. He marched up and introduced himself to me and immediately began making suggestions about how we ought to change what had already been done. His presence was distracting—not at all helpful.

It didn't take long for me to realize that Joel had some sort of behavioral disorder. He was intelligent but couldn't follow simple directions or join productively in a group activity. My facilitator antennae went up. I immediately began planning for how to keep Joel under control as the retreat progressed. Experience has taught me that a character like Joel can quickly spin things out of control.

The event got underway and, just as I suspected, Joel continued to act out in the larger group. I moved our activity from the larger group into smaller group work, where Joel would be less disruptive. I hovered around Joel's table to keep the other leaders at that table on task. The retreat seemed to be moving along nicely, despite Joel's disruptions.

Then, in the third hour, while small groups were deeply engaged in a dialogue experience, Joel approached me at the leadership podium. He was adamant.

"We have to pray, right now!" Joel exclaimed.

I tried to calm him by explaining that we were scheduled for a meditation moment after this small group activity concluded. I told Joel that he needed to return to his seat and let the retreat unfold in the way it had been designed.

"No, we need to pray now!" Joel was really starting to get agitated.

After my third round of arguments with Joel, something shifted in me. It wasn't alarm. It wasn't a need to control Joel's behavior. It was a moment of release. I recognized that Joel was operating from a deeper place of wisdom than I was operating from. I had been dismissing Joel because I thought he had to be handled. I thought I knew what needed to happen next in the room.

But I decided to unknow my plan and to see what might happen if I followed Joel's lead. I agreed to Joel's demand, and he returned to his seat.

I located the pastor of the congregation at one of the tables, and I asked him to come forward to lead a prayer. (I often do this when I am not certain that I can speak authentically in the prayer language of a congregation.) He led a large group prayer, and then I asked the individual tables to pray together for the life of the congregation and for our decision-making. At first, people were puzzled by the interruption of their group task and they were resistant to shift gears, but they eventually settled into their prayer assignment.

Then it happened. An amazing movement occurred within our gathering space. To this day I cannot fully explain the change, but there was a palpable altered energy. As the prayer time concluded, the tables returned to their work, and there was a buzz of creativity that had not been present before. Later, after the retreat, several leaders commented on the shift. Others recalled that the best planning insights of the day emerged in the time immediately following that prayer. People wanted to know how I had the wisdom to stop action and call for prayer. I told the leaders about Joel's faithful intervention.

During facilitation, and in the face of Joel's constant disruption, I had hunkered deeply into a stance of knowing, of wrestling an event into submission under my watchful eye. Joel was aware that I needed to unknow what would happen next. He challenged my stance until I listened. I continue to be grateful for Joel's faithful leadership at that retreat and the important lesson he taught me on that day.

Unknowing requires personal spiritual centeredness and confidence that God will lead if given the opportunity to do so. It requires the capacity to challenge long-established assumptions. It takes conviction that collective wisdom will emerge if given an opening to breathe. It requires courage to fail the expectations that others hold of you as one who fixes their problems.

How do we know when we have made the passage from knowing to unknowing? It is a destination at which we never fully arrive. Being cognizant of our own unknowing means, in fact, that we are still knowing. However, we are making progress when we manage to adopt a stance of wonder.

Wonder is the ability to suspend judgment and to hold competing thoughts and values in tension. Wonder arrives when we acknowledge that experience is always larger than our ability to interpret it. We hold our interpretations more loosely and ponder the interpretations of others. In a state of wonder, we perceive the organization from its edges and boundaries, rather than from the center. We develop a rich capacity for challenging unstated assumptions and seeing things with fresh eyes.

From Advocating to Attending

Energy follows attention. How we pay attention and what we focus on determines how decision-making unfolds. The quality of our attention shapes our steps and choices.

When people in the organization are anxious, leaders adopt an advocating stance. We decide what is right, and then we promote a course of action, a cause, a principle or goal. Advocacy is a set of actions targeted to support a particular outcome or policy. It is dogged and single-minded. We admire leaders who grab hold of a thing and won't let go, believing that this demonstrates tenacity and perspicacity. After all, inviting change in an institution requires fierce determination on the part of the leader. Or does it?

A liminal season is different from other seasons of change, because the level of disruption is so profound. In a liminal season we don't have a clear picture of where we are, nor do we have clarity about where we are going. We only know that a step in some direction is required to keep on learning. Advocacy doesn't serve us well when we are living with such profound disorientation. Advocacy assumes certainty about direction and clarity about outcomes.

By contrast, an attending stance invites me to love God and others in the situation directly in front of me. I avoid adopting an opinion, cause, principle, or targeted outcome. I embrace the fullness of the present moment for all that it might teach me. I open all my senses to experience the situation before me through the divine consciousness that dwells within it and within me.

Attending is a capacity for deep seeing and listening. It is an act of being fully present in the moment. It is not simply an act of hearing or remembering what was said and done. Attending is becoming fully awake to all that is happening, to the full potential within and around me.

My husband and I enjoy bicycling, and we often take biking vacations. Several years ago, we took a biking vacation to Maine through Acadia National Park. We are from the Midwest, which makes us flatlanders. The biking that I do throughout the year is limited to flat landscapes along old rail beds. I often fool myself into thinking that I am a decent cyclist until I encounter hilly terrain. Acadia National Park almost did me in. The gentle rolling hills described in the travel brochure were hyperbole. The hills before us were large and formidable. I was struggling.

Early in the ride I discovered a riding technique that worked for me on the hills. I found that I was easily discouraged by the size of a hill when I saw the enormity of it in front of me. So I learned to look down at the road beneath my feet when pedaling up a hill. I would count the number of revolutions of my pedals from one to ten, and then begin again. In this simple manner, I managed to stay in the moment and not get overwhelmed by what lay ahead.

Count to ten, begin again, just keep pedaling. It became my mantra. I never looked up, and in this manner, I conquered one hill after another.

It seemed to be working, and so I attached myself to this approach with ferocity. I blocked out everything else. Companion bikers would pedal up alongside of me and encourage me, "You're doing great! Keep going! Only a little further!" Others would pull alongside and give advice, "Why don't you try shifting into a different gear? It will work easier for you." I ignored all of them, kept my head down, and just kept pedaling. It began to rain.

The voice in my head was an advocating voice. *This is what works. Don't stray from the plan. Just keep on doing this thing that works* . . . until it simply didn't work anymore. My legs wouldn't complete a single additional rotation, and so I climbed off the bike, in defeat, soaked by the rain.

At that moment, a quiet voice somewhere in the back of my head whispered, "Look up!" I glanced up to witness a remarkable vista. In front of me was the verdant green crest of an enormous hill. Atop the hill was a quaint white lighthouse with a bright red roof. Arched from one side of the hill to the other, just over the top of the lighthouse, was a full rainbow, the likes of which I had never seen. A complete arc with every color of the spectrum, fully alive and dancing in the sunbeams that pierced the raindrops.

In that moment, the ridiculous nature of my advocating approach (look down and keep on pedaling) became fully apparent to me. I had almost missed this moment of awe and beauty. This was the thing I had signed on for, an experience in nature. And yet, in my sustained effort to master the goal of the ride, it almost passed me by. Had I looked up sooner, the beauty of the topography would have sustained me in my efforts.

The beauty and the majesty of the landscape broke through my defenses, and at once I was attendant to all that surrounded me. I was part of the terrain, it was part of me, and we were all part of God's magnificent creation. I suddenly saw the hills, the challenges, and my riding companions with fresh eyes. There were pine smells I hadn't noticed, textures on the hillside I had missed, and wildlife that had passed me by. In a moment I was transformed by the majesty of it all. I was awake and alive to my surroundings, able to see with fresh eyes and with an open heart. I was attending and full of love.

An advocating stance comes from a place of fear and reveals an absence of courage. When the uncertainty of the situation becomes too unwieldly, we wrestle it down to a manageable scale. We pretend to be in control by adopting a principle, position, or an approach to advance.

It is not a coincidence that my shift in stance happened in a moment of failure. When we come face to face with the limited capacity of our own efforts, we are suddenly open to a change in perspective, to seeing with fresh eyes, all that had previously been unseen. When failure breaks us open, we are ready to receive.

The same principle applies in leadership scenarios. Imagine a pastor is appointed to a new congregation by his bishop. In his most recent appointment, the pastor successfully led his congregation through the closing of their building and relocation to a more manageable campus. The new congregation to which he has been appointed is also struggling with the upkeep of their plant. The bishop has suggested that this congregation may also need to consider relocation.

The pastor quickly studies the situation and takes a position about the sale of the building. The right thing to do is to sell this property and move on, he advocates. He leads the people in this direction. He knows how to execute this move. He backs himself into a corner around this position until it becomes fully evident that the congregation is not ready to part with its property and isn't supporting him in his position. The congregation begins grumbling to the bishop and asking that the pastor be moved.

Only then, in a state of failed leadership, is the pastor able to wake up and attend to other possibilities. An opportunity presents itself to share the building with another congregation of a different ethnic background. The possibility of merging with a theologically like-minded neighboring congregation bubbles up organically. Until the leader sets aside his advocacy, he is not free to attend to an emerging option.

From Striving to Surrender

The striving self likes to power through barriers and get things resolved. The striving self is a false self. It doesn't know what it doesn't know. It can't see what might be possible if we let go of negative attachments and faulty goals. The striving self is vested in the ego self (the little self) of the leaders and the organization. The striving self needs to look good, feel competent, and appear successful.

The alternative—to surrender, in our present-day vernacular—has negative connotations: to give in, to give up, to concede defeat, to become inactive. Nobody wants to be that leader. However, abandoning hope and conceding defeat is not the form of surrender that I am describing here. I am invoking surrender in the sense that it is used within the contemplative tradition.

To surrender is to yield, to submit to the powerful reality of what is, to take a long loving look at what is real, to welcome the situation in front of you. Surrender means accepting the past for what it was, embracing the present reality, yielding to the mystery of the future and the mystery of God in that future. When I surrender, I accept my experience as something that must be, by necessity, so that I can learn what I need to learn, to become what I need to become, in order to embrace my future. [13]

Cross Pointe Meadows is a congregation that has fallen from grace, at least in its own eyes. Once a flagship church in the denomination, Cross Pointe offered nationally recognized programs, ran their own camp, and operated a day school. The staff of the church was a who's who of talent, and the congregation boasted a budget that consistently allocated 20 percent of operating income to missions.

A series of traumas befell the congregation, beginning ten years ago. First, there was the troubled departure of a much-loved leader, under a shadow of misconduct, followed by a theological debate that resulted in a church split and the loss of a third of the membership body. This was followed by several years of gradual but continued numerical decline.

Today Cross Pointe Meadows is a shadow of its former self, still a more than viable mid-sized congregation but one that lives under the cloud of its former reputation. Year after year the congregation downsizes its budget and struggles to maintain both the quantity and quality of its programs. The church is overstaffed, because it cannot bring itself to right-size programming expectations. After all, the programs of the church are what leaders pin their hopes to, attempting to restart growth and restore vitality. The physical plant is too large for the existing membership body but selling off property seems like giving up on a vision of growth. The leaders of Cross Pointe Meadows are discouraged and exhausted. The harder they strive and the more they envision, the less they seem to thrive.

The challenge that this congregation faces is not a leadership or managerial problem; it is a spiritual dilemma. The congregation needs to shift from a striving stance to a surrendering stance. The congregation must embrace the reality of its present size and capacity. The leaders of Cross Pointe are very resistant to this transition. To surrender feels like giving up and giving up is not a part of the DNA of Cross Pointe.

Making great efforts to achieve or attain something is admired in our culture. Indeed, it seems a basic part of the human condition that we struggle or fight vigorously to overcome barriers that stand in our way. We struggle, we labor, we do all that can be done, even when the odds are against us and losses seem inevitable. We make every possible effort, so that at the end of the day we can say, "I have done my best, my utmost. If the effort fails and the battle is lost, at least I did every conceivable thing that I could imagine. No one can accuse me of giving in or slacking off."

The problem with striving is that we erroneously place ourselves at the center of the equation. We form false attachments to actions of our own making. We imagine that it is all up to us and that the best of our efforts, skills, and imaginings will be enough to overcome the obstacles. We are like the Kansas peddler in Oz, hidden behind the control panel and trying to pass ourselves off as the great and powerful Wizard.

Richard Rohr says that the understanding of any situation begins with the primal "yes" of basic acceptance. We look at our present situation and assent to its confines. We avoid labeling or categorizing our situation as something inherently good or bad. We simply surrender and adapt to the reality of it. We cannot see or understand anything about our present challenges if we begin with, "No, we cannot allow this to happen."[14]

Cynthia Bourgeault, Episcopal priest, writer, and modern-day mystic, explains that surrender is not the same thing as "welcoming" the situation in front of us. Rather, it is yielding to what wants to emerge. We let go of our old understandings and negative attachments to the past. We release our fears and embrace the loss of ego, and then we approach the situation with an interior acceptance that allows new approaches and insights.[15]

A few years ago, my sister-in-law was diagnosed with early onset Alzheimer's disease. The diagnosis was devastating for our entire family, but it was intriguing to watch the response of family members and friends in response to the diagnosis. After the initial shock, some wanted to surrender, and others wanted to strive. The strivers wanted to confront and battle the disease. These individuals felt that it was best for my sister-in-law if she refused to blindly accept the diagnosis. This group advocated for fighting the diagnosis, for finding new doctors, for arguing with doctors over protocols, and for striving for positive outcomes. Their stance seemed admirable, but at the same time, fearful and exhausting.

My brother and sister-in-law chose a different route. They chose the route of surrender, and it was beautiful and inspiring. Relatively quickly, they accepted the reality that my sister-in-law had the disease. In many ways it was a relief for them to finally receive a diagnosis, because the daily symptoms had become quite alarming. Some might view this as a sign of weakness on their part. It wasn't. Their surrender was an act of incredible bravery.

Their surrender did not result in either passivity or inactivity. They yielded to the reality of their situation. This yielding empowered them in ways that soon became apparent. They were able to make decisions about finances and where to live as the disease progressed, while my sister-in-law still had the capacity to participate in those decisions. They were able to find the best doctors and discover cutting-edge programs that they knew would help them cope with a life altered by Alzheimer's. My sister-in-law became a national spokesperson for the Alzheimer's Association in the early stages of her disease, which allowed her to proactively use her lifelong skills as a gifted public speaker.

In short, their surrender to the inevitability of the disease allowed them to participate generatively in the unfolding of their future. "We did not choose to have this disease, it chose us," my brother said. "But I choose it back," he went on to say. "I choose this experience for everything that it can teach me about myself and our future." This statement is the essence of a surrendering stance and of the generativity that lies on the other side of surrender.

Only after surrender can we be led by our own emerging future. Congregations today need to surrender to the realities of decline and stagnation. We need to quit fighting our liminal reality, as if this is something that we can ward off by striving harder at what we know how to do. By saying yes to what is, we can align ourselves with a future that needs and wants to emerge through us.

No one masters the art of leading with Presence. It is an ideal to which we aspire, knowing that remarkable things happen in the life of an organization whose leaders manifest Presence with some consistency. On our best days, we gain a glimmer of what it requires of us and what we must surrender. On our worst days, we are anxious, reactive, clingy, and without a clue about how to right our spiritual stance. We take two small steps forward, and then one giant step back.

The good news is that the grace of God covers it all. We simply need to keep putting one foot in front of the other, engaging the journey that emerges. In the end, Presence is a gift of God. Our hope is that we are self-aware enough to step aside and receive the gift when it is given. And then, in the words of the great Christian theologian and mystic Julian of Norwich, "All shall be well, and all shall be well, and all manner of thing shall be well."

NOTES

1. Richard Rohr, "What Sustains Me: Contemplation," *Sojourners*, June 15, 2009. https://sojo.net/articles/what-sustains-me-contemplation. Accessed December 27, 2018.

2. Claus Otto Scharmer, "The Blind Spot of Leadership: Presencing as a Social Technology of Freedom," April 2003. http://www.ottoscharmer.com/publications/articles.

3. Although this quote is often attributed to Frankl, the quote is not found in any of Frankl's published works. The quote was popularized by motivational author Stephen R. Covey; however, Covey disclaims authorship.

4. Claus Otto Scharmer, *Theory U: Leading from the Future as It Emerges* (second edition) (Oakland, CA: Berrett-Koehler Publishers, 2016), 117–18.

5. Tilden Edwards, *Embracing the Call to Spiritual Depth: Gifts for Contemplative Living* (Mahwah, NJ: Paulist Press, 2010), 1–6.

6. Ronald Heifetz, Alexander Grashow, and Marty Linsky, *The Practice of Adaptive Leadership: Tools and Tactics for Changing Your Organization and the World* (Boston, MA: Harvard Business Press, 2009), 7–9.

7. Thomas Merton, *New Seeds of Contemplation* (Boston, MA: Shambhala Publications, 2003), 36.

8. Merton, *New Seeds of Contemplation*, 37.

9. James Bacik, "Thomas Merton on the True Self," *June Reflections*. 2015;38(10). http://frjimbacik.org/wp-content/uploads/2015/06/reflections-june-2015-merton-on-true-self1.pdf.

10. Scharmer, *Theory U*, 40–42.

11. Scharmer, *Theory U*, 43–44.

12. Edwards, *Embracing the Call to Spiritual Depth*, 6.

13. William Barry, S.J., *Paying Attention to God: Discernment in Prayer* (Notre Dame, IN: Ave Maria Press, 1990), 46–51.

14. Richard Rohr, *The Naked Now: Learning to See as the Mystics See* (New York: The Crossroads Publishing Company, 2009), 55–58.

15. Cynthia Bourgault, *Relearning Surrender* (Victoria, BC: The Contemplative Society, 2012).

Chapter Three

Tending the Soul of the Institution

Finding Soul in Place

There is in all visible things an invisible fecundity, a dimmed light, a meek namelessness, a hidden wholeness.
—Thomas Merton (Hagia Sophia)

Many of the practices that we associate with "good" leadership don't serve us well in a liminal season. Casting a clear vision isn't advisable when we can't see the future with reasonable certainty. Demonstrating personal conviction isn't possible when we don't know what to feel convicted about. Strengthening others by sharing power can be dangerous when you don't know whom to strengthen. Building commitment to action and achieving small wins—again, not helpful if you don't know which actions or wins would benefit the organization. So, what is a leader to do?

In the last chapter, we explored the presence that serves a leader well during a liminal season. However, the leader must also *do* something with their presence. A leader who doesn't offer some meaningful work for the organization to do will not remain in leadership long. Followers tolerate ambiguity and inactivity only so long before they attach themselves elsewhere. Any charismatic individual who offers an alternative to anxiety will capture their attention.

Which activities are helpful for an organization in a liminal season? Deepening the discernment skills of the leadership body (chapter 4). Shaping institutional memory to help people make meaning of their experience (chapter 5). Clarifying the organization's purpose now (chapter 6). Engaging emergence (chapter 7). All of these are productive activities for liminal seasons.

The shared characteristic of each of these practices is that they are not driven by human knowledge or personal striving. They are grounded in listening to the authentic self of the institution and letting the self of the institution guide the decision-making of leaders for a season. In short, good organizational work in a liminal season involves tending the soul of the institution. On the surface, these activities mirror leadership actions taken in times of certainty. Upon deeper reflection, these are activities deeply rooted in unknowing, attending, and surrender.

A leader tending the soul of the institution is like a piano tuner working with a tuning fork. A piano tuner strikes the fork to produce an authentic pitch. She listens for how that pitch resonates with the same note struck on the piano. If the piano is out of tune, she hears a distinct warble between the note played on the piano and the note played by the tuning fork; the further apart the warbles, the more out of tune the piano. By either tightening or loosening the piano's strings, she can reduce the warble until it's in line with the tuning fork.

A leader working with the soul of the institution is listening for resonance between a proposed course of action and the true self of the organization. She brings a variety of tools along to help her listen for the resonance. She tweaks a proposed course of action until she feels comfortable that the way forward aligns with the authentic self of the organization.

Soul-tending work begins with a basic assumption—that an organization has a soul—a spark of divine essence that represents the true self of the organization. Furthermore, this work assumes that God is invested in the choices that impact the future of the organization, and that God will reveal God's interest to those with discerning hearts. Finally, this work assumes that discernment is the key to connecting the authentic self of the leader with the authentic self of the institution. These are big assumptions that need to be unpacked before we delve further into institutional soul-tending work.

WHAT IS THE SOUL?

Evelyn Underhill, poet, writer, and mystic, describes the soul as a transmitting instrument that recognizes the fundamental relationship between itself and the divine. She quotes Ignatius in saying, "What matters most to soul is the full realization that: We come from God. We belong to God. We are destined for God."[1] The work of the soul, then, is the challenge of discerning: To what or whom do we belong? Where have we come from? Where are we destined to go next?

Wisdom teacher and writer Cynthia Bourgeault describes the soul as the deepest source of our true and authentic self, the agent of divine guidance, the eternal principle present when we came into life. The voice of soul has an intuitive sense of integrity, coherence, and elegance. It responds to beauty and to wonder.[2]

American author and psychologist James Hillman writes: "The soul of each of us is given a unique *daimon*[3] before we are born, and it has selected an image or pattern that we live on earth. The daimon remembers what is in your image and belongs to your pattern, and therefore your daimon is the carrier of your destiny."[4]

But what about the presence of soul in an institutional setting? Does an organization have a daimon—a God-given essence or calling? Does an organization have a true self, an agent of divine guidance that can help leaders distinguish authenticity from inauthenticity?

In my consulting work with congregations, I have encountered a divine essence at work in the life of institutions—something that longs to express itself in moments of direction setting and decision-making. For many years, I resisted using soul language to describe this essence. Soul language felt overused and at times misused. I feared that it was theologically incorrect to speak of an organization as having a soul, that soul language could only apply to the human experience.

So I adopted many other labels to describe the divine essence to which I had been witness. I talked about the movement of the Spirit through the organization. I described it as a distinct part of the organizational culture, the spirituality of the people, or the collective voice of the leadership body. In the end, each of these labels failed me. None of these constructs adequately describe the essence, and none of these labels help me approach the essence as an agent of guidance. So, by default, I find myself returning to the notion that an institution has a soul, and I find companionship in others who have named the same.

Distinguished psychiatrist, spiritual counselor, and author Gerald G. May reflects on the soulfulness of institutions in his work *The Dark Night of the Soul*:

> Any grouping of people is more than the sum of its parts; it is a system with its own life, an entity in many ways like a person. Each family, community, church, business, even nation or culture has characteristics and experiences that constitute a life of its own. Like the individuals who make them up, groups can be seen as growing and learning, yearning and dreaming, decaying and dying. An obvious question in this context is whether social systems might be said to have (or be) souls. . . . If a group derives its being, energy, and characteristics from the mutual interactions of its constituents, then it can be said to have at least some soul qualities.[5]

In *Unmasking the Powers*, Walter Wink, professor of biblical theology, references the "angels of the churches" in the Book of Revelations. The seven letters addressed to the seven churches in Asia Minor are each inscribed to the Angel of the church—as opposed to the people or the leaders of the church. Wink points out that the angels are not something separate from the church but represent the wholeness of the church. The angels are more than a mere personification of the church; the angels represent the totality of the people, their history, their vocation, their personality, and their destiny.[6] Although Wink doesn't use the word soul, he does emphasize the existence of a divine essence. There is something more that encompasses and surpasses all other ways of understanding these gathered communities.

If an organization or institution (I am using these two terms interchangeably throughout this chapter) has a soul, then it behooves us to learn how to regard it, respect it, and work with it. We cannot presume to strengthen an organization, its culture, its processes, its structures without engaging its soulfulness. The remainder of this book is about doing just that—learning to regard and engage the soul of the institution.

Attempting to define "soul" is presumptuous, because soul is primarily mystery. However, we need some shared language to ground our conversation. I offer the following definition—a work in progress to be sure—but a starting place from which to begin our dialogue:

> *The soul is an agent of the divine spark in the institution. The soul is the authentic and truest self of the institution; the source of its divine calling, character, and destiny; the protector of institutional integrity.*

WHAT THE SOUL IS NOT

When my children were very small, a favorite bedtime story was *Are You My Mother?* by P. D. Eastman. The story begins with a baby bird hatching from its egg. Unsure of its identity, the bird goes off in search of a mother. He encounters a kitten, a chicken, a dog, a cow, a boat, an airplane, and eventually a steam shovel. In each instance he mistakenly assumes that the thing he encounters is his mother. The hilarity of the story grows as the tiny bird identifies with progressively larger unrelated species. In the end, the baby bird discovers his mother and his own identity by ruling out all the things that she is not.

My journey toward the soulfulness of institutions has mirrored Eastman's story. I have settled into using institutional soul language by discovering what it is not. The soul finds expression in several organizational constructs, but these expressions of the soul are not the soul. The soul is not the collective voice of the leadership body, the culture of the organization, the spirituality of the organization, nor is it the movement of the Holy Spirit through the organization. The soul is closely related to these phenomena, and may find expression through them, but the divine essence is not contained by these things.

Soul Is Not the Collective Leadership Voice

In a spiritually healthy organization, leaders are in communion with the divine essence of the organization and make choices that honor the truest part of the institution. There is an authenticity in the organization that its leaders intuitively nurture, even when they don't understand the source of that authenticity. We call this wisdom.

However, we must be careful not to conclude that the collective voice of the leadership body is the same thing as the voice of the soul. The soul will have its own voice. Leaders may discern that voice, they may make decisions on behalf of that voice, but they can't claim to be that voice.

Institutional soul has been on a journey that precedes the journey of the present leadership body. Leaders may understand the soul's journey within the institution, and they may be asked to speak on its behalf, but the expression of the collective human experience in the present institution is not necessarily the same as the expression of the institution's soul.

Consider the following illustration which distinguishes between the decision-making voice of a leadership body and the practice of discerning with the soul of the institution. First Presbyterian Church is considering a proposal recently submitted to the church by the city. The proposal is for weekday rental of the church parking lot. The proposal seeks to create additional parking spaces for city workers. Leaders of Session (the congregation's governing board) debate the opportunity and decide that the proposal has enough merit to bring it forward for congregational vote. A congregational meeting is called to order. The pastor opens with a perfunctory prayer. Those gathered debate the advantages and disadvantages of accepting the city's proposal, carefully following Robert's Rules of Order to keep conflict at bay.

Most attendees sit quietly and listen to the proceedings. A handful of vocal members debate the safety and security issues, as well as the expected effect on church activities. They consider the financial implications and the impact on the congregation's insurance coverage. After thirty minutes of debate someone calls for a vote. The proposal is narrowly voted down. Later, leaders reflect that the possible benefits did not outweigh the hassles introduced by the parking proposal.

This decision-making exercise was an expression of the best thinking of the membership body. Leaders relied on their personal knowledge and brought common sense to bear on the choice. They decided on behalf of the organization. It was not an engagement with institutional soul.

Now, consider an alternative. A small group of leaders gathers to discern with the soul of the institution. They too explore the pros and cons of the proposal. They carefully consider the known financial and fiduciary implications. Then the group moves into prayer and silence. Group members take time to acknowledge their personal preferences, doing their best to name the biases that shape their preferences. One group member acknowledges a recent personal conflict with the mayor that left a sour taste for the city in her mouth. Another group member acknowledges a personal relationship with the city commissioner that may be influencing his perspective. The group prays together to be released from these personal biases so that their discernment can focus on the good of the whole.

The group evaluates the connection between the parking lot decision and the mission of the congregation. They examine each of the congregation's core values, seeking to discern how the proposal advances or diminishes each value in the life of the congregation. They imagine how this decision connects to the larger story of the congregation's relationship to the city. They pay attention to the longing and the resistance emerging in their hearts and minds. The group works by consensus, ensuring that each member is heard and that all reservations are addressed. Again, they rest in silence—attending to any lingering unsettledness.

Somewhere during this discernment, a collective awareness emerges that the congregation's well-being is inexorably tied to the well-being of the city and its workers. Group leaders sense a mutual longing to honor the congregation's symbiotic relationship with the city by accepting the city's proposed parking relationship. Their discernment honors something that transcends the logic of the collective leadership body. Their discernment creates space for the soul of the institution to speak.

The process used by this leadership body wasn't mysterious. One might argue that these leaders simply took time to ground their decision-making in the core values of the congregation. However, the intentionality that these leaders formed through prayer, stillness, and shedding their personal agendas was transformative. Their intentions changed this from a simple group decision-making exercise into a discernment with the voice of soul.

Soul Is Not Holy Spirit Movement

Spirit is disembodied, transient, and illusive. Spirit is aspirational, noble, and unbound by time and space. Spirit moves through an organization, infusing leaders, structure, and processes with divine light and energy. The movement of the Spirit in the organization is a powerful and awe-inspiring thing, but it is different from the divine essence that resides within the institution. The soul is rooted in the context, memory, and vocation of a specific place. It is fully embodied in this time, this space, and these people. Soul may be infused by Spirit, but it is not the same thing as Spirit.

In the second chapter of the book of Acts, the Holy Spirit arrives in the upper room where Jesus' disciples are gathered. The movement of the Spirit on Pentecost was so powerful that those gathered began to speak in other languages, as the Spirit gave them ability. The movement of Spirit through the upper room on Pentecost originated from outside of the gathered body. It was beyond them, moved through them, and transformed them. It was not resident within the gathered community.

I've had the privilege of witnessing Holy Spirit movement in my work with congregations. When the Spirit moves, profound things happen—often creating a sharp break from the past or changing the trajectory of leadership action. People are headed in one direction or find themselves stuck in a place of indecision. Through the movement of the Spirit they find new energy and clarity of direction.

In contrast, the soul of the institution is resident in the organization. It lives in the context of a people and place, much like a human soul abides within the human body. The soul can mediate the movement of the Spirit, and it can interpret the movement of the Spirit. The soul is not the Spirit.

A recent decision made at People's Church illustrates the difference. People's Church has always taken an academic approach to adult faith formation. For decades, adult faith formation relied on the use of outside experts, visiting theologians, and retired seminary professors to teach faith formation classes. Lately, diminishing resources have curtailed the use of outside teachers. Members have not felt equipped to step in as adult Sunday school leaders. With insufficient funds to bring in outside speakers, most adult Sunday school classes have folded.

Leaders have turned to small group ministry as an alternative model of faith formation. They believe that small groups will advance faith formation while also nurturing intimacy in the congregation. They believe that small groups will more effectively serve the needs of People's Church today. The congregation is responding well to its nascent small group ministry. There is a spirit of renewal and revival afoot.

Unexpectantly, a wealthy donor is moved to offer the church a significant financial gift, a gift he claims to be making at the prompting of the Holy Spirit. The donor has earmarked the gift to launch a theological institute. The gift will allow the congregation to bring in nationally prominent thinkers, speakers, and teachers once again.

Accepting the grant seems like a no-brainer to the leaders of the congregation. Who would look such a gift horse in the mouth? No one stops to question whether the gift should be accepted, to consider the impact that the grant will have on small group ministry. The church swiftly reverts to its "hired expert" approach to faith formation. And it feels like something small has died. A spark of warmth, energy, and engagement at People's Church smolders and then burns out. Something new that was longing for expression was ignored in service to a compulsive attraction to the past.

I have no doubt that the Holy Spirit was at work in the life of this individual donor. His generosity was prompted by something that moved him. That movement is impacting the church. However, there was no effort on the part of leaders to help the donor evaluate or shape the impulse. They grabbed at the money. Sometimes, what appears to be a remarkable spirit-led opportunity really isn't in the best interest of soul. What unintended consequences might this gift deliver? Would the donor support any other use of these funds? The congregation moved in response to Spirit in the life of an individual, without considering the needs of institutional soul.

Soul Is Not Organizational Culture

Edgar Schein, a professor of management at the Massachusetts Institute of Technology and the author of several books on organizational culture, defines organizational culture as "a pattern of shared assumptions learned by a group as it solves its problems of external adaptation and internal integration, . . . which are taught to new members as the correct way to perceive, think, and feel in relation to those problems."[7] The culture of an organization typically informs how information is shared, decisions are made, leadership is recognized, and conflicts are resolved.

The culture of an institution is alive, vibrant, and evolving, much like the soul. It manifests in the collective whole, and it has a stable nature, much like soul does. However, Schein's definition reminds us that culture is formed in response to something else. Culture is not the source of anything. It is a patterned response developed over time.

In a healthy congregation, culture will mirror the divine essence. For example, a congregation whose divine spark embraces inclusivity creates a culture that is collaborative. Alternatively, culture may restrict the free expression of soul. Let's imagine that the same congregation calls a pastor with an autocratic, directive style of leadership. His leadership doesn't resonate with the inclusive soul of the organization and the congregation languishes as a result.

New Hope Baptist Church recently merged with SALT, an independent evangelical church. New Hope could no longer afford to maintain their historic building. Membership had been in decline for over twenty years. The membership body was aging, and leaders didn't have the energy or creativity to pursue revitalization.

SALT had been renting building space from New Hope for several years. SALT members were primarily young families with children. They had no permanent worship space and no place to house their growing ministry. They didn't have enough money to purchase their own ministry site, and many things about the New Hope location and physical plant appealed to them.

The merger of the two churches looked great on paper. Each congregation was missing a generation of members. Together, they formed a multi-generational community. The theologies and political orientations of the two congregations were well aligned. There were some differences in governance, but leaders were eventually able to reconcile those differences.

Prior to the merger, leaders worked hard to shape a culture that both congregations might embrace. Members of the newly combined congregation signed a behavioral covenant together. They wrote a new set of core values to live by.

It all worked well, until it didn't. Within three years of the merger, most of the New Hope members had left the church. When asked why, departing members said that the merged congregation didn't feel like their church—it just didn't feel like home. Their long-standing core values of soul liberty and soul freedom, which are hallmarks of Baptist identity, had slipped through the cracks. The new pastor operated with greater authority than they were accustomed to. He led with a directive leadership style that made them uncomfortable.

It could be that the members of the original New Hope congregation just couldn't adapt, that they were resistant to change. There is probably some truth to that. However, it is also likely that the merged congregation retained the soulful essence of the original SALT community and lost the soulful essence of New Hope.

The troubled merger of New Hope and SALT is a lesson in the difficulty of combining church cultures. But it is an equally important lesson in the need for soul-tending work in mergers. No amount of work on the culture of the merged church could offset the sense that the soul of New Hope had been abandoned.

Soul Is Not Spirituality

Mary Anne Huddleston, author and spiritual director, defines spirituality as "the manner, mode, or way in which an individual or a group lives out its doctrines, ideas, values, hopes, traditions and habits of faith."[8]

A faith-based organization has many ways to express its spirituality. Each expression grows from a conscious quest for God in the collective human experience. Ritual, worship, sacraments, and prayer practices are obvious expressions of spirituality in institutional life.

Corrine Ware, professor of theology at the Episcopal Seminary of the Southwest, names four styles of spirituality: thinking, feeling, being, doing. She applies these styles to individuals as well as congregations.[9] Ware explains that each faith community has its own preferred type of spirituality, represented by some blending of the four basic types. Most congregations express a strong preference for one or two types of spirituality and a lesser attachment to the other styles.

Congregations that favor a head, or "thinking," spirituality are attracted to sermons, lectures, and study as a way of experiencing God. These congregations value understanding ideas about God. They value the written word and sound doctrine. They demonstrate a love of order and desire for things to be rational and logical. Their experience of God comes from considering the truth of God with their minds.

Congregations with a heart spirituality know God by "feeling" God's presence. A congregation that favors this spirituality type over the others will experience highs and lows in religious feelings. Witness and proclamation are important to them. Heart spirituality is most often engaged through spontaneous experiences, through music, testimony, and more informal worship styles.

A congregation with a "being" spirituality values the journey. In fact, the quest is more important than an arrival. Being is more important than doing. This spiritual type values a mystical approach to God. They enjoy pausing to listen for God or wondering at God's creation. This congregation enjoys contemplation, wordless prayer, and experiences of silence and stillness.

Finally, some congregations embrace a spirituality of "doing." These congregations experience God's presence best when they are actively working to advance a cause for which they are passionate. They are rooted in social concerns and are often impatient with the passivity of the other types.

In a healthy congregation, the spirituality of a congregation is an expression of the soul, but it is not the soul itself. In fact, a congregation can grow unhealthy by practicing a spirituality that is not an authentic reflection of its soul.

Consider All Saints church. Thirty years ago, the church called a charismatic preacher. He stayed for ten years. With his arrival, the spirituality of All Saints began to shift in dramatic ways. This pastor honed the intellectualism of the congregation, often to the exclusion of the feeling, being, and doing aspects of the congregation's spirituality. The congregation became less about heart and more about head; less about wisdom and more about knowledge; less about mystery and more about God engaged through study.

By the end of his tenure, worship attendance was at an all-time high, but the congregation's spirituality and soul had withered. The congregation lost its warm feeling as a place to belong and lost its attachment to the pursuit of social justice. At the time, leaders weren't much concerned about the shifts, because their preacher was packing the people in on Sunday mornings.

The charismatic pastor departed abruptly after ten years of service. Within one year of the pastor's departure, worship attendance dropped by 25 percent. The exodus of congregants continued for five years, and today the congregation is one-third the size it was during that glory era.

Congregants look back to that era with great longing. Oh, to be that impactful once again. However, leaders also acknowledge the hollowness of that time, in every other aspect of congregational life outside of the pulpit. The "head" spirituality of the congregation emphasized during that era did not honor the soul of the congregation. Today, leaders are working to restore a well-rounded spirituality that they believe is more authentic to the soul of their congregation.

Do the Distinctions Really Matter?

By now, you may very well be asking, "What difference do all of these distinctions make?" For the last several decades, I don't think these distinctions made much of a difference in faith-based institutions. In the past, we built organizations that were spiritually open, relationally healthy, and organizationally strong, and the soul of the institution simply thrived. It wasn't important to name the distinctions between soul, culture, spirit, and spirituality. It was all part of a functioning whole and the soul quietly did its work.

Today, the Church and the institutions that make up the Church are in a liminal state. An era of thriving has come to an end, and a new way of being is not yet clear. Congregations are closing faster than we can plant new ones. Seminaries are failing. Denominational structures are imploding. We are struggling to stay alive and relevant. Too many congregations have lost their ability to innovate. Too many are spiritually dead. Relationships are increasingly dysfunctional. Structures and cultures are overgrown and bureaucratic. We can no longer simply take institutional soul for granted.

In response to the chaos, pastoral leaders are working harder and faster. Staff teams are exhausted, chasing a proliferation of programs that they hope will save their congregation from extinction. Middle judicatory bodies[10] search for fresh programs, new worship styles, and innovative discipleship approaches that seem to be working somewhere in some context. They repackage these approaches and advocate or impose them universally on all congregations under their jurisdiction. Frantic local leaders latch on to generic programs and implement them without first considering context and soul. If it doesn't work here, at least I won't appear to be standing idly by, fiddling while Rome burns.

Our striving is futile. Each time that we carelessly impose an attempt at revitalization, one that isn't right for our context, we wound the soul of the institution. Each of the illustrations shared earlier in this chapter tell the tale of well-intentioned leadership groups making decisions on behalf of the organization, while failing to honor the soul of the congregation. When we fail to listen to the soul of the institution, we diminish it.

If the soul is the authentic and truest self of the institution; the source of its divine calling, character, and destiny; the protector of institutional integrity—then wounding the soul diminishes the integrity and the authenticity of the organization. Without integrity and authenticity, vitality is not possible.

THE SOUL'S JOURNEY

All biological beings are born, we mature and grow through adolescence, we become somewhat sedentary adults, we decline in old age, and we die. Numerous scholars have noticed how congregations mimic the life cycle of biological organisms.[11] Congregations exhibit predictable behavioral patterns and encounter predictable leadership challenges based on their stage in the developmental life cycle. Demonstrating this life cycle and helping a church locate itself en route between life and death has become an important tool for helping churches revitalize.[12]

How is the congregation's developmental life cycle related to the soul of the institution? Is every organization birthed with a soul, or only religious organizations? When does soul arrive? Does the organization's soul die when the organization dies?

These are great questions, and I have no idea how to answer them. Intuitively, it makes sense that institutional soul accompanies the organization throughout its developmental life cycle. There are seasons when the soul is more easily accessible to us as an expression of the most authentic self of the organization. There are other seasons when the soul seems diminished and much more difficult to access. Along the way, leaders take actions that wound the soul, and other actions that heal earlier wounds.

John H. Mostyn works as a spiritual director alongside institutions. John points out that the inspirational insight that gives birth to an organization is clearest when the organization comes into being. Over time, changing leadership, changing needs, and changing perceptions result in the divine spark getting blurred or lost. The farther an organization gets from the original point of inspiration, the more difficult it is for leaders to identify with that original expression of divine essence. And yet a spark remains, even when everything else seems to have changed: the demographics of the community, the culture of religion, and the passion and skills of congregants. Hence the need for constant and systematic reorientations toward the soul. This search for clarity usually goes by the name of discernment. It is the act of making the divine spark clearer to the people who are choosing the direction of the institution now.[13]

In my soul-tending work with organizations, I have adopted the following terms to help leaders dialogue about the journey of soul in the life of their institutions. You might consider using these terms to talk about the journey of soul within your organization.

- *Divine Spark:* A pure expression of the divine vocation of the institution, unencumbered by institutional memory. Pure wisdom.
- *Founding Vision:* A possible indicator of the divine spark of the soul. An idea is born, experiments are undertaken and learned from, resources are

allocated, and an organization is established. The vision, vocation, and values of the organization are in near alignment with the vision and values of the leader. The culture and the spirituality are pure expressions of the divine spark.

However, we must bear in mind that not all founding visions are an expression of the divine spark. For example, some congregations are born as the result of a church split. A church split may be the result of the soul longing for more authentic expression, an essence that couldn't find voice in the prior congregation. Most church splits, however, are the convoluted result of people behaving badly and wounding one another. As a result, a divine spark is hidden at the time of birth and must be coaxed forward in a later season.

- *Leadership Transitions:* With each generational shift in leadership the organization becomes increasingly removed from the simplicity of the founding vision. Each generation of leaders adds a new layer of interpretation. It becomes increasingly difficult to access the founding vision, but fresh expressions of the divine spark emerge along the way.
- *Wounding and Strengthening:* In each era, the soul of the institution experiences seasons of wounding and strengthening. Sin, betrayal, misconduct, pride, shame, cynicism, and fear are layered into the life of the institution, clouding the energy and strength of the divine spark. A congregation experiences three successive senior pastors who engage in sexual misconduct while in office. These collective experiences wound the soul of the institution and the soul must be healed. (See chapter 5 for more about memory shaping as a healing activity for the soul.)
- *Dark Nights and Glory Eras:* The institution experiences seasons of life during which God appears to be absent from the work of the institution, and the organization languishes. Alternately, other seasons of work and ministry feel richly Spirit-led, bearing fruit and producing new growth.
- *Liminal Seasons:* Seasons when the organization is naturally more receptive to rediscovering and working with the divine essence. During these seasons people are ready to work on shaping the narrative and clarifying purpose. The chapter that follows a liminal season is often marked by a greater sense of purpose and direction, with clearer access to the divine essence.

Institutional soul tending seeks resonance between the divine spark and the actions of the present membership body. We work with the soul through our everyday work, what the membership body does together. Through the teaching, healing, planning, and management of the organization. The soul is not above or below these things. The soul is in these things.

APPROACHING THE SOUL OF THE INSTITUTION

When I finally acknowledged the presence of soul in institutions, I felt compelled to change the way I entered my client systems. I committed to arriving early, or creating space early in my work schedule, to simply sit in the sanctuary or public meeting space to pray. I asked God to reveal something to me about the soul of the organization that I was about to engage. Absolutely nothing happened. I began to wonder, again, if institutional soul was just a figment of my imagination.

Eventually, I came to realize that I was approaching soul too directly. After all, I would never sit face to face with you upon our first meeting and demand that you tell me something about your soul. Likely, you wouldn't know how to respond to my query if I did ask. And I wouldn't know how to observe the soul within you. I might notice some things about your personality or spirituality. We might discuss your temperament or Enneagram. We might even talk about your prayer life or your worship practice. But none of that would describe your soul.

The soul in humans and in institutions is illusive. Maybe that is why the only way I have been able to describe it to you is by naming what it is not. The soul is mystery. We cannot observe or describe institutional soul directly. We can only see evidence of its existence. My early attempts to observe the soul of the institution remind me of Moses' bold demand to see God's glory, in the book of Exodus, Chapter 33 (NIV):

> [18] Then Moses said, "Now show me your glory."
>
> [19] And the LORD said, "I will cause all my goodness to pass in front of you, and I will proclaim my name, the LORD, in your presence. I will have mercy on whom I will have mercy, and I will have compassion on whom I will have compassion. [20] But," he said, "you cannot see my face, for no one may see me and live."
>
> [21] Then the LORD said, "There is a place near me where you may stand on a rock. [22] When my glory passes by, I will put you in a cleft in the rock and cover you with my hand until I have passed by. [23] Then I will remove my hand and you will see my back; but my face must not be seen."

If the soul is the agent of the divine spark in the institution, then one might expect the divine spark to behave like divine glory. We cannot witness or engage it directly, we can only watch from the cleft, should soul pass by.

Author, educator, and activist Parker Palmer described both the shyness and the tenacity of the soul in his book *A Hidden Wholeness*:

> The soul is like a wild animal . . . tough, resilient, resourceful, savvy, and self-sufficient: it knows how to survive in hard places. . . . Yet despite its toughness, the soul is also shy. Just like a wild animal, it seeks safety in the dense underbrush, especially when other people are around. If we want to see a wild

animal, we know that the last thing we should do is go crashing through the woods yelling for it to come out. But if we will walk quietly into the woods, sit patiently at the base of a tree, breathe with the earth, and fade into our surroundings, the wild creature we seek might put in an appearance. We may see it only briefly and only out of the corner of an eye—but the sight is a gift we will always treasure as an end in itself. [14]

Eventually, I came to appreciate that I could not go crashing around the organizations I worked with demanding soul to reveal itself to me. I had to sit more quietly with leaders and coax it forward, watch for it to pass by, invite it to reveal itself through silence, prayer, and discernment. Sometimes I think we catch a glimmer of it, oftentimes not.

If we can't witness the soul, how in the world are we supposed to work with it? How can we nurture it? More importantly, how can we let it nurture us?

There are a variety of soulful practices that faith-based organizations can do to tend the soul of the leader alongside the soul of the institution, important practices like worship, prayer, and spiritual discipline. This book is not about those things, simply because those are not the areas of organizational life to which I tend. I will leave those topics to others more qualified.

My interest lies in four bodies of soulful organizational work that I find helpful in liminal seasons: deepening group discernment (chapter 4), shaping institutional memory (chapter 5), clarifying purpose (chapter 6), and engaging emergence (chapter 7). These bodies of work are group work, not individual undertakings. These works engage the soul of the institution as an agent of divine guidance. The remaining chapters of this book will address each of these soulful group practices in turn.

ELIMINATING A FALSE DIVIDE

One of the greatest barriers to soul-tending work is a false dualism we perpetuate, the separation of organizational leadership and spiritual leadership. We put our best spiritual leaders in deacon-type roles and ask them to tend the spiritual, educational, and pastoral life of the organization. We put our best fiduciary and strategic thinkers in the role of board leaders or trustees, and we ask them to take care of the organization. In doing this, we create a dualistic leadership system. You are either an organizational type or a spiritual type.

Richard Rohr explains the dualistic nature of the human brain.

The dualistic mind is essentially binary, either/or thinking. It knows by comparison, opposition, and differentiation. It uses descriptive words like good/evil, pretty/ugly, smart/stupid, not realizing there may be a hundred degrees between the two ends of each spectrum. Dualistic thinking works well for the sake of simplification and conversation, but not for the sake of truth or the immense subtlety of actual personal experience. Most of us settle for quick and easy answers instead of any deep perception, which we leave to poets, philosophers, and prophets.[15]

Leaders of faith-based institutions want their organizations to be effective, efficient, and soulful. Unfortunately, we tend to nurture effectiveness and efficiency and ignore the leadership skills that nurture soulfulness.

We must select leaders for our governing boards that have some capacity for soul-tending work. We must nurture their abilities by developing the disciplines of discernment. We must select facilitation tools and meeting management techniques that foster open mind, heart, and spirit. This is the subject of our next chapter.

Be forewarned. Congregations that introduce soul-tending work at the board level often experience a radical transformation of their leadership body. Some individuals who have served in leadership for years will suddenly step out of service because soul-tending work doesn't suit them. Others who have clung to the margins of the organization will suddenly be attracted to leadership for the first time because they find soul-tending work deeply satisfying. Many who serve in leadership will report that their personal spiritual lives have been enriched by their engagement with the soul of the institution.

These changes don't typically happen smoothly. There are bumps and bruises along the way as some members feel disenfranchised by the changes and others feel emboldened. Some will feel that the organization has taken a dangerous turn. Others will feel that things are moving in the right direction at last.

Tending the soul of the institution is an ongoing process, a journey without an identifiable conclusion. There isn't a right way or a wrong way to do this work. It is difficult to know where you are on the path, or even if you are on the path. The work belongs to the community; you cannot do it alone. These features make soul-tending work both dangerous and full of opportunity—much like the times that we live in.

NOTES

1. Evelyn Underhill, *The Ways of the Spirit* (New York: Crossroads, 1997), 116.
2. This definition is taken from from an online course offered by the *Contemplative Journal*, "Four Voices Method of Discernment," facilitated by Cynthia Bourgeault, May–June of 2015.
3. In Greek mythology daimons could be either good or evil. The good daimons were considered to be guardian spirits, giving guidance and protection to the ones they watched over.
4. James Hillman, *The Soul's Code: In Search of Character and Calling* (New York: Random House, 1996).

5. Gerald C. May, *The Dark Night of the Soul: A Psychiatrist Explores the Connection Between Darkness and Spiritual Growth* (New York: Harper Collins, 2005), 176.

6. Walter Wink, *Unmasking the Powers: The Invisible Forces That Determine Human Existence* (Philadelphia, PA: Fortress Press, 1986), 70–71.

7. Edgar H. Schein, *Organizational Culture and Leadership* (fourth edition) (San Francisco, CA: Jossey-Bass, 2010), 18.

8. Mary Anne Huddleston, *Springs of Spirituality* (Ligouri, MO: Triumph Books, 1995), 20.

9. Corrine Ware, *Discover Your Spiritual Type* (Lanham, MD: Rowman & Littlefield, 2014), 35–40.

10. A middle judicatory body is the administrative structure or organization found in religious denominations between the local congregation and the widest or highest national or international level. For example, the middle judicatory body in the United Methodist Church is referred to as a Conference. In the Presbyterian Church it is the Presbytery. In the Lutheran Church it is called the Synod.

11. For various interpretations of the congregational life cycle, see Martin F. Saarinen, *The Life Cycle of a Congregation* (Washington, DC: Alban Institute, 1986); Arlin J. Rothauge, *The Life Cycle in Congregations: A Process of Natural Creation and an Opportunity for New Creation* (New York: Episcopal Church Center, 1994); Alice Mann, *Can Our Church Live?: Redeveloping Congregations in Decline* (Bethesda, MD: Alban Institute, 1999).

12. Alban at Duke Divinity School. *From Birth to Death: Exploring the Life Cycle of the Church*. Posted on August 11, 2006. Accessed December 10, 2018.

13. John H. Mostyn, "Transforming Institutions: God's Call—A Director's Response," in *Tending the Holy: Spiritual Direction Across Traditions*, edited by Norvene Vest (New York: Morehouse Publishing, 2003).

14. Parker Palmer, *A Hidden Wholeness* (San Francisco, CA: Jossey-Bass—A Wiley Imprint, 2004), 58–59.

15. Richard Rohr, "The Dualistic Mind," *The Center for Action and Contemplation Newsletter* originally published on January 29, 2017. Accessed on December 11, 2018.

Chapter Four

Deepening Group Discernment

Seeing What God Is Up To

God does not exist to answer our prayers, but by our prayers we come to discern the mind of God.
—Oswald Chambers

The leadership retreat was ending. We had used our time to design a planning process for the congregation—a process that would incorporate group discernment. We practiced several group discernment exercises together. It had been, I thought, a productive and meaningful day of work.

As I was preparing to take my leave, one leader sheepishly approached me and asked for a word. We stepped to the side of the room to ensure a more private conversation. "I'm rather embarrassed to ask this," he said, "but what exactly is discernment? I have heard this word my whole life in the church and we used it all day here, but no one has ever explained discernment to me in a way that I understand. What am I doing when I discern, especially when I do so on behalf of the congregation?"

This man was bright, articulate, and a lifelong churchgoer. He had served in church leadership for many years and participated actively in the day's work. Yet, here he was telling me at the *end* of our time together that he didn't understand the basic premise of our work.

Were my facilitation skills so poor that I had failed to instruct the group in the foundational principles of our work? I hastily explained discernment to him again, as clearly as I knew how, but he still looked puzzled. You see, he had never had a personal experience of being led by God—not one that he could name.

The weekend left me unsettled. Similar experiences in later months confirmed a slow-growing realization. As the Church, we have forgotten our discernment tradition. Our centuries-old practices of discernment feel foreign and out of place in our religious institutions. We have replaced discernment with rational decision-making. Those who practice discernment are often viewed suspiciously as "new age" touchy-feely types.

Since then, I have redoubled my own learning and efforts. I have developed richer practices for helping leaders tap into wisdom. It isn't easy. Discernment doesn't happen on demand, and most leaders prefer the familiar and predictable practices of decision-making, debate, and parliamentary procedure over the unfamiliar disciplines associated with sacred listening. It's not that they don't trust God to speak; they simply don't trust themselves to hear.

Our facility with prayer, silence, and stillness is so underdeveloped that leaders can't imagine God might be speaking *to them*. Others don't trust individual spiritual experience. They have been taught that the Bible is our only trustworthy source of revelation, or that ordained church leaders are the only qualified interpreters of Holy Spirit movement.

Our discomfort is understandable. The term "discern" in common parlance has been secularized, removing any sense of divine action. In daily usage discernment means to make a good choice using sound judgment. It is synonymous with being discriminating, judicious, shrewd, and clever. A discerning person is one who understands people, situations, and things clearly. Defaulting to this understanding of discernment, church leaders simply look to their most perceptive and discriminating leaders to make decisions on behalf of the whole.

This was precisely the definition of discernment that the leader in my opening story brought into our gathering. He couldn't imagine discernment as anything other than well-facilitated group decision-making, with a prayer thrown in on the side for good measure.

WHAT IS DISCERNMENT?

Ruth Haley Barton defines discernment as an ever-increasing capacity to "see" the work of God in the midst of the human situation, so that we can align ourselves with whatever God is doing. Discernment is a quality of attentiveness to God that, over time, develops our sense of God's heart and purpose in the moment. In communal discernment, we move beyond the personal to see what God is up to within the collective whole.[1]

Danny Morris and Chuck Olsen write, "To discern is to see through to the essence of a matter. Discernment distinguishes the real from the phony, the true from the false, the good from the evil, and the path toward God from the path away from God."[2]

If we believe that God is an active agent in the world, then we need practices for attending to God's agency. Most of the literature dealing with discernment addresses the practice of individual discernment. There are few resources related to group discernment in organizational settings. In this chapter, we will be exploring the challenges of working with group discernment, particularly during times of high anxiety and uncertainty. I will be using the terms "group," "communal," and "collective" interchangeably in reference to the discernment work of a community. We will explore a variety of questions. How is group discernment different from group decision-making? How do we prepare and equip leaders to discern on behalf of the whole? What practices best support communal discernment?

THE COMMUNAL DISCERNMENT TRADITION

The practice of discernment has deep roots within the Judeo-Christian tradition. The term discernment doesn't often appear in the Hebrew scriptures, but the idea of discernment is everywhere. King Solomon at the beginning of his reign pleaded with God, "Give your servant therefore an understanding mind to govern your people, that I may discern between good and evil, for who is able to govern this your great people?" (1 Kings 3:9).

From Solomon to the judges and prophets, God's leaders look for evidence of God's agency in the world and they seek to join their efforts with the movement of God. The story of Elisha in I Kings 19 illustrates such seeking.

> [11][The LORD] said, "Go out and stand on the mountain before the LORD, for the LORD is about to pass by." Now there was a great wind, so strong that it was splitting mountains and breaking rocks in pieces before the LORD, but the LORD was not in the wind; and after the wind an earthquake, but the LORD was not in the earthquake; [12]and after the earthquake a fire, but the LORD was not in the fire; and after the fire a sound of sheer silence. [13]When Elijah heard it, he wrapped his face in his mantle and went out and stood at the entrance of the cave. Then there came a voice to him that said, "What are you doing here, Elijah?"

In the Christian scriptures, the first collective discernment appears in Acts 15. The early church is engaged in debate about the need for Gentile followers to observe the circumcision and food rituals of the Jews. Paul and Barnabas bring this quandary to the council of apostles and elders in Jerusalem. The council deliberates together until they can say with one voice, "It seemed good to the Holy Spirit and to us" (Acts 15:28) to eliminate the burden of Jewish law on the Gentile converts, except for a few basic provisions.

Discernment has been addressed as a discipline in every century of church history since. In the early chapters of the church, the focus of discernment was primarily personal, not communal. From Origen in the first century to Cassian in the fourth century and Climacus in the sixth century, church theologians have grappled with what it means to discern God's will.[3]

When the Eastern Church and the Western Church diverged, the approach to discernment diverged as well. The Orthodox Church in the east looked to the mystics and the ascetics as guides in personal discernment, and they relied on the office of the bishop to discern on behalf of the institution. The Orthodox Church, emphasizing a strong trinitarian experience of God, elevated respect for the movement of the Holy Spirit and maintained a strong emphasis on discernment practices.

The Western Church, heavily influenced by the Roman Empire, adapted itself to the patterns of Roman law and deliberation. As a result of this adaptation, the Western Church lost some of the richness of its personal discernment traditions. The cardinals, as the primary authority figures in the church, became the primary guardians of discernment. The practice of personal discernment was subject to the authority, tradition, unity, and continuity of church officials. Even monastic communities deferred to the abbot or abbess as the final decision-maker, although the wisdom of the community remained important in shaping the leader's decisions.

The Dark Ages brought us Meister Eckhart, Thomas à Kempis, and other mystics who restored a personal and practical piety that the common man could relate to.

In the early sixteenth century, Ignatius of Loyola crafted the Spiritual Exercises, which outlined "Rules for the Discernment of Spirits." The rules blended imagination with reason, biblical connection, experience, and testing of the spirits by attending to feelings. This era also brought us the writings of John of the Cross and Teresa of Avila, stressing the importance of human yearning and the desires of the heart as discernment tools.

During the Protestant Reformation, Scripture was elevated as the most important tool for discerning God's will. John Calvin accentuated piety and order in discernment. Calvin's reliance on rules and ordinances shaped the way many of us approach group discernment today by creating group decision-making bodies authorized to decide on behalf of the whole.

The Anabaptist tradition modeled its congregations after the New Testament churches. This tradition emphasized the importance of every voice in discernment, minimizing hierarchical authority. The Quaker stream of this tradition is noteworthy for its emphasis on silence and the use of consensus and clearness committees as discernment disciplines.

The Methodist movement gave us what is now referred to as the Methodist quadrilateral to illuminate discernment—the balancing of (1) Scripture, (2) tradition, (3) reason, and (4) experience to determine the truth of an idea, theological interpretation, or lived event.

Today, we are witnessing the decline of institutional religion and a resurgent interest in spirituality. Our culture is increasingly interested in meditation and mindfulness. Mindfulness is the ability to be fully present and aware of where we are and what we are doing, to not be overly reactive or overwhelmed by what is going on around us. Meditation trains the mind to stay present and calm in the moment, ultimately creating long-lasting changes in the brain and promoting positive mental health habits. The growing interest in meditation and mindfulness, along with the confluence of Eastern and Western religious traditions, is reawakening an interest in discernment.

Although an interest in discernment is on the rise, the ancient tools of the practice remain largely unknown to our congregants. We need to rediscover our own praxis.

DECIDING VERSUS DISCERNING

"This is a congregation, not a business." If only I had a dollar for every time a leader made this bold assertion in my presence. Typically, right after making this claim, the same leader goes on to conduct the meeting at hand exactly as if the church were a business. Oh, yes, someone begins by offering a five-minute reflection followed by a prayer, but then we move into decision-making mode, the primary mode from which businesses operate.

We form an agenda. We load the agenda with problems to be solved or decisions to be made. For each agenda item, we frame a problem statement or decision query, name the underlying issues, propose a solution, argue the pros and cons, deal with the outliers, call for a vote, record the outcome, and move on. This is decision-making.

Decision-making is grounded in logical thinking and rational discourse. Decision-making assumes that we have the capacity to understand and solve our own problems and that this works best by maximizing available resources and maintaining order.

Group decision-making gathers leaders to debate organizational outcomes. Decisions are made as leaders work to resolve their differences, negotiating an outcome that will be acceptable to the whole—hopefully for the good of the whole.

Traditional meeting management disciplines like Robert's Rules of Order are designed to promote effective decision-making by minimizing conflict and promoting reasoned resolution to problems. Sometimes, these practices succumb to political tradeoffs, power plays, and a rush to judgment. Frequently the group divides into winning and losing factions, with residual feelings of triumph and failure. At its worst, group decision-making results in people pooling their collective ignorance.

Discernment is different. In group discernment, participants adopt a stance of indifference to anything but the will of the divine as discovered by the group, setting aside matters of ego, politics, opinion, or personal interest.

Discernment seeks out more than simple group agreement. The goal of discernment is to tap into the will and movement of the Holy Spirit. Sometimes that movement is felt palpably within a group—when a sense of divine Presence settles over the group in silence. Sometimes it is experienced more joyfully through a mutual sense of peace and rightness. Or it may manifest as a corporate sense of freedom, goodness, wholeness, healing, and reconciliation.[4]

Decision-making and discernment are closely enough related that leaders often fail to recognize the subtle boundaries between them. Both decision-making and discernment require effective processes and the choice of the right tools for the situation. Those processes and tools differ in some important ways, as outlined in table 4.1 on the next page.

In most institutional settings, the practicalities of leadership call for a blend of decision-making and discernment. Pure discernment happens according to the leading of the Spirit and in the fullness of God's time, not in accordance with our calendars and agendas. Often, organizations have very real deadlines that require action, such as finalizing a budget or approving a plan. So we create space for discernment, but we are cognizant of when decisions must be made in service to organizational deadlines.

A Discernment at North Pointe

The leaders of North Pointe Church gathered for a weekend of dialogue about the social justice platform of the congregation. The congregation had a long-standing commitment to social justice, but leaders were sensing a need for greater clarity about strategy.

Some in the congregation wanted to define the strategy broadly. This group saw the church as an incubator, a place nurturing the social justice consciousness of each member. They believed that every member should choose his or her own cause. They did not want their church to elevate a single social justice issue, because they feared that doing so would create insiders and outsiders—those who embraced the congregation's platform versus those who didn't.

Another constituency believed the congregation would be more impactful by pursuing a common cause and marshaling all the resources of the congregation to advance that cause. Many in this group wanted the church to focus

Table 4.1. Decision-Making versus Discernment

A Deciding Approach	A Discerning Approach
Assumptions	**Assumptions**
• Most problems are solvable if approached carefully and logically.	• God is not neutral about our mission or our choices.
• We have the capacity to understand and solve our own problems and embrace our own opportunities.	• God is self-disclosing.
• Maximizing the use of available resources is important.	• The Holy Spirit is our indwelling and ongoing guide.
• Maintaining or restoring order is important.	• Openness of spirit and attitude is required.
	• God's will is revealed in community.
Process	**Process**
• Defining the problem	• Framing the issue for discernment
• Looking for root causes	• Grounding it in core values and guiding principles
• Gathering the data	• Shedding ego and biases
• Interpreting the data	• Listening for the promptings of spirit
• Brainstorming alternatives/options	• Exploring our options
• Establishing decision criteria	• Weighing
• Evaluating alternatives	• Closing; moving toward selection
• Assessing risk and return	• Testing the decision with rest
• Selecting an optimal solution	
Tools	**Tools**
• Parliamentary procedures	• Consensus
• Majority rule	• Prayer/silence
• Root cause analysis	• Scripture
• Decision trees	• Listening circles
• Decision models	• Appreciative inquiry
• Probability scenarios	• Storytelling
• Simulations	• Clearness committees
	• Consolation/desolation
Who Does the Work?	**Who Does the Work?**
• Authorized leaders on behalf of the whole	• All invested parties

on eliminating racism. Adopting racism as a focus would require significant changes in staffing and worship practices.

Still others had their own specific social justice issues that they were hoping to promote in the weekend of dialogue: homelessness, fair trade, and the refugee crisis. They agreed with narrowing the platform but didn't want racism to be the single focal point.

We began a weekend of discernment. We taught participants to distinguish between decision-making and discernment, and we asked them to maintain a discerning mindset.

We agreed that no decisions would be made at this event. Rather, we would steep ourselves in prayer and test to see if consensus was rising at the end of the weekend. We made time for individual reflection, small group conversation, and large group dialogue. Silence and song were invited spontaneously in response to the spirit in the room.

A tug of war between decision-making and discernment was evident in the room throughout the weekend. Beautiful moments emerged as people set aside personal agendas and listened to the ideas of another. There were other moments, particularly when the issue of race was on the table, when polarization reared its ugly head and participants adopted a striving and advocating stance. It was palpable when the group lost their sense of freedom and wonder (a discerning stance) and moved toward advocacy and posturing for a specific outcome (a deciding stance).

Each time we noticed the room shifting toward a deciding stance, we stopped action. We invited prayer, silence, or song. The music director taught us two complementary songs. We learned to sing them first individually, and then we layered them together in rounds. We sang over and over, listening carefully to each other until the chords and verses wound themselves together in our heads and hearts. We began to sing with one voice. The unified spirit we discovered in our vocal exercise stayed with us as we engaged in discernment.

Toward the close of our time together, we considered possible future directions. We brainstormed our possible options and followed that with a simple polling exercise to test for consensus. Each participant received five sticky dots. The dots represented the available energy and resources of the congregation. Each participant was invited to "spend" their dots on the options that best reflected their yearning for the future of the congregation.

Remarkably, the dot exercise revealed consensus emerging in support of an anti-racism platform. It became visually clear that the issue of race was compelling for all in attendance. Once the racial justice "champions" set aside their strident advocacy stance, others were able to join them in discerning a mutual sense of passion and interest.

PREPARING A COMMUNITY FOR DISCERNMENT

It takes a lot of preparation and intentionality to shift a community from the practice of decision-making to the practice of discernment. Preparing a community for discernment begins by exploring the community's assumptions about God's agency in the world. Then leaders must be recruited who demonstrate the right competencies—those behavioral attributes, skills, and abilities that support a discerning mindset. Next, recruited leaders are taught how to cultivate stillness through prayer and meditation. Finally, an intentional group discernment processes is designed to guide their collective work.

The preparation is time-consuming, but it need not be overwhelming. Every small effort can make a substantial impact. As leaders strengthen their discernment muscles, they develop a different leadership presence and naturally yearn for a new leadership approach.

Explore Assumptions

We experience God through action. We reflect on how God has acted in our lives, and we make meaning of our experience. Over time, the meanings we make become a paradigm of faith, a personal theology through which we interpret all subsequent experience. Problematically, we might blindly accept our theology as universal truth.

Discernment makes no inherent sense to people who believe that God set the world in motion and then stepped back to see how humans negotiate things on their own. These people won't be able to consider God as an active agent in decision-making. Similarly, people who believe that God's will prevails regardless of the actions we take are not likely to see discernment as a purposeful activity.

Preparing leaders for group discernment involves helping them explore their assumptions about God's agency—and this may take a substantial amount of time. Following are some of the theological assumptions that support a practice of group discernment. A group doesn't have to completely agree with these precepts to embrace group discernment. However, they do need to develop clarity about their theological stance, so that a discernment process can be designed that aligns with their theology.

1. *God is self-revealing.* God's yearning for relationship with humankind is a consistent theme in Scripture. "I will take you as my people, and I will be your God. You shall know that I am" (Genesis 6:7). In Deut. 30:11 we are reminded that the knowledge of God is not far and unreachable, but "very near to you; it is in your mouth and in your heart for you to observe." God is self-disclosing to us in the ongoing act of creation, in the unfolding of history, in the person of Jesus, and through the indwelling of the Holy Spirit.

2. *God gives us choice, and the choices we make matter to God.* God is not indifferent to what we do in our faith lives or within our faith communities. God cares about the daily decisions that shape the soul of our religious institutions. "I have set before you life and death, blessings and curses. Choose life so that you and your descendants may live, loving the Lord your God, obeying him, and holding fast to him" (Deut. 30:19–20).

3. *Discernment is a gift from God, mediated through the presence of the Holy Spirit.* Our very ability to discern is a gift, promised to us by Jesus, moderated by the Holy Spirit. "The Holy Spirit, whom the Father will send in my name, will teach you everything, and remind you of all that I have said to you" (John 14:26). Paul also cites the discernment of spirits as one of the gifts of the Spirit given for the common good (1 Cor. 12:4–10).

4. *Discernment is a discipline we practice.* Through grace we are given the gift of discernment, but the practice of discernment requires ongoing discipline and engagement. Putting on the mind of Christ (Phil. 2:5; 1 Cor. 2:14), we strengthen our ability to know the will of God. Each time we engage a discernment process, we strengthen our spiritual muscles and deepen our collective wisdom.

5. *The truths of God are revealed and tested within community.* We are meant for life in community. We are one body with many members, and all the members are required for the body to function properly. "To each is given the manifestation of the Spirit for the common good. To one is given the gift of utterance of wisdom, and to another the utterance of knowledge according to the same Spirit" (1 Cor. 12:7–8). Left on our own, we are prone to misinterpret the spirits according to our personal will and liking. The community helps us to test our discernment, because the community manifests collective wisdom.

6. *Discernment unfolds in God's time.* We can initiate a practice of discernment, but the leading of the Spirit cannot be manipulated in accordance with our timelines. The Spirit leads in *kairos* time, the fullness of God's time. Therefore, we must exercise patience and forbearance with one another and God, as we wait for clarity to emerge. "I wait for the Lord, my soul waits, and in his word, I hope" (Psalm 130:5).

Exploring the theological assumptions of the group is the first stage in building readiness for group discernment. It is critical and ongoing. Leaders may need to revisit these assumptions repeatedly as they deepen their discernment practice. As new leaders rotate onto the board, the assumptions must be reexplored. Only then can we begin to develop the skills, abilities, and competencies of the discerners—those who have been chosen to lead.

Build Competency

A group of leaders gathered to name the core values of their congregation. The core values were going to be used to shape a new ministry model for the congregation, a reorientation toward multi-site ministry. Instead of being one church in one location, the congregation was preparing to become one church at three locations. Leaders thought it important to shape a set of unified core values to yoke the three campuses together.

We framed the work to be done, and I laid out a discernment approach. We began with a guided meditation that invited deep breathing, silence, and mental imagery. I led the exercise with *my* eyes closed to connect with my spiritual center, seeking to be fully open to both God and the group as I facilitated their work.

Halfway through the five-minute exercise it occurred to me that I should open my eyes to better gauge the energy of the room. What I saw was unsettling. About a third of the room emanated a deep sense of prayerful engagement. Another third seemed to be trying, but the uncomfortable, squirming body language indicated they were highly agitated by the experience and couldn't wait for it to be over. The final third was either staring blankly into space, waiting to get back to some "real" work, or they had pulled out their mobile devices as a cure for their boredom. Two-thirds of the group could not tolerate five minutes of silence—they couldn't find their way to stillness!

Once upon a time, I would have taken this as an indictment against my facilitation skills. If I were better at leading prayer, people would not be so disengaged and impatient. This is partially true—I could do a much better job at leading meditation. However, in time, I have also come to appreciate that people have little capacity for stillness. The practice of sitting quietly with God is foreign to most. Leaders cannot be good discerners if they are not comfortable with stillness.

We can't build our competency in group discernment unless we have leaders who are spiritually awake. Unfortunately, in practice we often appoint leaders without considering their spiritual maturity. We nominate trustees because of their financial and legal acumen. We ask our best strategic thinkers to engage in planning on our behalf. We recruit human resource specialists to serve on our personnel committees. We put compassionate and caring people on the deacon board. We pause to consider whether our appointees are emotionally stable individuals, but we rarely consider spiritual depth. And then, perhaps, we pick an extra person to serve on each team as a spiritual anchor, someone who can pray on our behalf and remind us of the spiritual dimension of our work from time to time. Or we delegate that task to the clergy leader in the room.

Alternatively, and equally problematic, we assemble a group of prayer warriors who have no organizational acumen and ask them to make operational decisions. Such a group may engage in prayer without shaping any pragmatic organizational outcomes.

I have also seen congregations mistakenly place these two groups alongside one another in a parallel process. The organizational leaders gather together in one room to make operational decisions. The prayer warriors gather in a neighboring room to bathe the process in prayer. There is no bridge created between the two groups. The deciders never ask to hear how the prayers are feeling led. Those praying don't engage the organizational dimensions of the problem they are praying about.

We need both organizational savvy and spiritual maturity within the leadership body. We need organizationally strong leaders with deep spiritual rootedness who are open to what might emerge from the practice of discernment.

Collective discernment must begin with attending to the spiritual competencies of the leadership body. A congregation seeking to plan may need an intentional season of preparation in which leaders hone their discernment skills before discerning on behalf of the whole. Bear in mind that moving a leadership body toward a discerning mindset is a culture shift for most congregations. Every generation of leaders must be trained and retrained. Eventually one generation of leaders will begin to model the behavior for future generations to follow. Eventually, a discerning orientation will filter its way through the organization. It takes the time that it takes.

There is often a lowest common denominator at work in groups gathered for collective discernment. The quality of the work in the room degenerates to the level of the least spiritually mature person in the room. In some instances, the least competent person will be timid and quietly observe the discernment of the larger group. Their lack of spiritual maturity may have little impact on the larger group. However, this also means that their voice is excluded from the discernment process, because they are too intimidated to join in. Whatever the Spirit may have intended for them to receive is lost to us.

The more common outcome is that the immature leader grows uncomfortable during the discernment practice. He or she acts out, spewing his or her own anxiety into the room and sidetracking the rest of the group. The only way to overcome this condition is by ensuring that we invite spiritually mature leaders into the process and that we continually strengthen the discernment muscles of each member in the group—including the pastor.

Following are some descriptions of the competencies we are seeking to cultivate, the qualities that will support the work of discernment.[5] Bear in mind that no individual possesses all these qualities. These are idealized guideposts to help shape our conversation about spiritual maturity.

> *Sagacity:* Displays concern for others; considers the advice of others; deals well with a variety of people; learns from others; is thoughtful, fair, and a good listener; is not afraid to admit mistakes, correct mistakes, and moves on.
>
> *Discriminating:* Able to distinguish between truth and error, right and wrong; demonstrates good judgment; acts within his or her own physi-

cal, emotional, and intellectual limitations; is sensible; thinks before speaking, acting, or making decisions.

Perspicacity: Demonstrates insight and intuition, a keen observer of mental and spiritual acuity; can see through things, read between the lines; can understand and interpret the environment.

Reasoning: Has a logical mind; can apply knowledge to a situation; can distinguish between the long or the short view; makes meaningful connections between ideas and concepts; is able to make clear choices and act upon them.

Contemplative Awareness: Is awake to the movement of spirit within self, others, and the organization; prayerful; is comfortable with silence, stillness, and waiting; adopts an orientation of spiritual wonder and awe for the sacredness of life; embraces unity in all things; stays fully present to what is unfolding now.

Cultivate Stillness

The right competencies will equip a leader for the work of discernment. However, something more is required. The discerning leader must be able to access stillness and encourage it in others.

Communal discernment involves listening for the One true voice and learning to distinguish that voice from the other voices that clamor for attention.[6] Our ability to discern is dependent upon the quality of our attention, on our capacity for stillness, our ability to quiet our minds and disassociate from the constant chatter in our brains.

Stillness is an open state of readiness, awe, and wonder that undergirds a discernment process. Stillness is the condition achieved when we settle into an unknowing, attending, and surrendering stance described in chapter 2 of this book.

Inner stillness is associated with an environment of silence and solitude. In silence, we create a quiet place to give our full attention to God. In solitude, we withdraw from the busyness of our lives and the company of others. We pull back and create space to give God access to our souls. Jesus repeatedly used silence and solitude to deepen his capacity for stillness. "He would withdraw to deserted places and pray" (Luke 5:16).

Silence and solitude make way for stillness, but they don't ensure a state of stillness. We can be outwardly silent and still be haunted by our own inner chatter. We can be outwardly alone and yet accompanied by a gaggle of competing inner voices.

Leaders must be taught how to approach stillness. It doesn't work well to simply dump people into silence, because they don't know what to do with their own internal chatter. This is where spiritual practices come into the picture. Practices like guided meditation, slow and repetitive reading of scripture, journaling, purposeful walks, and working with modeling clay or other art supplies give the mind, hands, and body something to do on one level, while inviting stillness on a spiritual level.

Deepen Prayer Practices

The typical devotional prayer that precedes many of our board and committee meetings is not helpful to group discernment. A board meeting is called to order and the pastor is asked to provide an opening prayer. The pastor's offering includes a scripture verse, followed by a wordy reflection on the passage. It is a beautiful and inspiring invocation, filled with rich phrases and evocative theological ideas.

Wordy prayers rarely invite stillness. They give us lots to think about, but stillness is not about thinking. If we want to invite people into a discerning mindset, we need to reexamine the way we pray. An ancient prayer classification uses two Greek words that feel clumsy but are quite useful for our purposes.

Kataphatic prayer is content based, built on the positive assertions we make about God. It uses words, images, symbols, and ideas to approach God. We take elements of what we believe to be true and offer those ideas and thoughts to God. Litanies, creeds, guided reflections, and spoken intercessions are all examples of this form of prayer. The pastor's opening devotion in the meeting described previously was kataphatic prayer.

Apophatic prayer is content free. We empty our minds of words and ideas, simply resting in the presence of God with us. We acknowledge that God is bigger than our knowing, greater than our capacity to describe. Apophatic prayer rests in pure experience. Breath prayers, silent meditation, centering prayer, and body prayer are all examples of the apophatic tradition.

Both forms of prayer are inherently good. Each honors God, but each stimulates a different part of the brain. Kataphatic prayers stimulate the left side of the brain. These prayers engage our objective, logical, and analytical response. Groups who approach their work with word-based content prayers reinforce rational thinking. Kataphatic prayer serves decision-making well.

Apophatic prayers engage the right side of the brain. The right side of the brain is where we perceive and synthesize the wholeness of things. The right side of the brain is where we intuit religious experience and, hence, where we interpret the movement of Spirit. If discernment is our goal, then emptying prayer is a better entry point. A group that grounds its work in wordless prayer is more likely to open itself to the mystery and movement of God when considering alternatives and making choices.

In the previous example, following the pastor's wordy opening prayer, members of the board were asked to choose between two possible tenants for rental space in their building. The group immediately gravitated toward decision-making. They discussed all that they logically knew about the rental situation. They asserted the pros and cons of each alternative. They advocated on behalf of various special interest groups in the congregation. In the end, they made a rational decision, but would we describe their process as a discernment? Did board members orient themselves to the soul of the institution or to the mind and will of God? Probably not. It was an amalgam of their best efforts, offered up to God. Worthy work perhaps, but not discernment.

DESIGNING A COMMUNAL DISCERNMENT PROCESS

Marge shows up to the church council meeting, excited about a revelation she believes she received during her personal prayer time. When given the opportunity to speak, Marge clutches her Bible to her chest, declaring that God told her the congregation needs to buy new carpeting for the sanctuary. The rest of the Council sits in stunned silence trying to figure out what to do with Marge and her personal prayer revelation. How do they respect Marge's personal experience and still hold it up for scrutiny? How do they decide if this is even an issue worthy of discernment?

Group discernment doesn't occur spontaneously. It requires structure and process. Without good process, all manner of human dysfunction may find its way into the conversational mix. We need a process that attends to the mystery of the Holy while minimizing the foibles of human bias and self-interest

Thomas H. Green says, "Discernment can easily be a polite and pious name for a 'tyranny of the majority,' a way of attaching God's name and authority to what most of the group want, or believe he [*sic*] must want. If this happens, then, as we have seen, 'discernment' becomes a way of manipulating God to agree with our convictions concerning action and decision making."[7]

Without a skeletal framework for the process, a group is likely to wander unproductively. Differentiating between the preferences of one and the needs of the whole creates apprehension. Distinguishing between the true and false selves of the institution makes us feel unsettled. We need a container to hold our anxiety, while we tend to the Holy.

My husband's British grandmother taught me the importance of good process when she taught me how to prepare a proper cup of tea. Like many Americans, I thought nothing of sticking a cup of water into the microwave, plopping in a tea bag, and calling it done. I valued speed over process. I didn't realize how tepid the result was until I enjoyed the full-bodied taste of tea prepared the proper way.

The proper way to brew tea is to bring a kettle of water to a full boil, keeping it over the heat until the kettle whistles. Meanwhile, a separate brewing pot is preheated by filling it with hot tap water and letting the pot rest until the kettle boils. The tepid water in the brewing pot is emptied once the kettle begins to whistle. The tea bags are inserted in the bottom of the empty brewing pot. The boiling water from the kettle is poured over the tea bags in the brewing pot and the tea is steeped for a full three to five minutes before serving. The tea bags are removed before drinking the tea. The heat of the water and the length of the steep will vary from one tea to the next, but careful attention to the overall process is critical.

The extra time and attention required to prepare a proper tea is rewarded with noticeably fuller flavor. Discernment is similar. The process at first seems cumbersome and painstakingly slow, but when honored, it fosters rich dialogue. With time and practice, discerners settle into natural discernment rhythms, eventually developing a practice that is seamless and elegant.

The discernment process outlined in the following is adapted from Danny Morris and Charles Olsen in their book *Discerning God's Will Together*. The quality of group discernment improves as we master a basic flow that involves eight distinct steps that we will explore later: framing, grounding, shedding, listening, exploring, choosing, closing, and testing. Eventually, we learn to move seamlessly through each stage, doubling back when needed, skipping stages as appropriate, all without getting bogged down in the framework itself. The movements are not meant to be mechanical. They are fluid. The sequence of the movements varies depending on context.

The Role of Leader

Before we explore the phases of communal discernment, it is important to note that the process benefits from good facilitation. Someone must monitor the flow of work and the dynamics of the group. You cannot put a group of leaders together in a room and expect that they will organically negotiate their way through a discernment process. There are too many potential sidetracks and distractions that can take a group off course. The facilitator isn't put "in charge" of the people in the room, but the facilitator does need authority to guide the process.

The designation of *moderator* is sometimes given to the person who guides a majority-rule decision-making process. This is typically someone well acquainted with Robert's Rules of Order or some other group decision-making discipline. The individual asked to lead a communal process of discernment may be referred to as a *discernmentarian*. A discernmentarian is a group spiritual guide who is well acquainted with the movements of discernment and the spiritual disciplines that help participants progress through the movements.[8]

The authorized leader of a group (i.e., the chairperson or moderator) can fulfill the role of discernmentarian, provided he or she is equipped with the spiritual guidance tools. Any member of the group may be asked to serve in the role of discernmentarian, although it is important that the person chosen be free from attachment to outcomes and capable of recognizing when the rest of the group has been captured by anxiety or bias. For this reason, on important discernment topics, groups often bring in an outsider to serve as discernmentarian. The outsider doesn't have an investment in the outcomes and is better able to identify and address hidden assumptions and biases.

Framing

The first phase of the discernment process is framing. The framing of the decision, problem, or issue invites the group to carefully consider the boundaries of their work. What is this about, and what is this not about? How broad or how narrow are the boundaries of the conversation? What is on the table and what is off the table for dialogue purposes?

The leaders at Stonecrest Community Church are concerned about a decline in weekend worship attendance. Worship attendance has decreased by 5 percent each year for the past five years, although membership, giving, and the average annual pledge continue to grow. Overall, the congregation feels vibrant and alive, yet leaders are worried by this decline in worship attendance. Leaders know that Stonecrest's worship decline is consistent with a larger national trend, but they wonder what, if anything, they should be doing about it.

Every month the topic is listed on the governing board's meeting agenda as "worship attendance." Every month, leaders spend fifteen to twenty minutes brainstorming/worrying about the decline in attendance, without ever deciding whether there is a problem with worship, and if there is, what the nature of the problem might be, and what action might be called for. After months of this fruitless activity, board leaders decide to engage in a more intentional discernment process.

Their first task is to figure out how to frame the discernment topic. There are several valid ways to frame this topic, with each frame inviting a different conversational focus. The leaders at Stonecrest discussed the following possible frames.

- What are we being invited to attend to in the decline of worship attendance?
- What is the future of worship at Stonecrest Church?
- How will discipleship in our congregation change if people worship with less frequency?
- Should we add a worship service to better meet the needs of our community?

• How might we reach out to millennials through the worship ministry of our congregation?

You can see how differently the conversation would unfold under each frame. Each framing has something to do with the topic of declining worship, but each frame emphasizes a different aspect of the problem. For this reason, the framing of the issue is often a discernment unto itself and will often take as much time as the entire rest of the discernment process. Whatever the subject, the discernment question needs to be clearly stated and agreed upon by the group.

Leaders at Stonecrest decided to begin their discernment process broadly, working with this framing question: "What is the future of worship at Stonecrest Community Church?" They knew that they could narrow the question as the discernment unfolded, and they didn't want their early conversation to be too limiting or to rest on unstated assumptions about the causes of worship decline. They also wanted to avoid the scarcity mentality that might accompany a conversation framed solely around declining attendance.

Grounding

Every discernment process needs to be grounded in guiding principle(s) that are important to the discerning body. The guiding principle(s) should be relevant to the issue and should help to create meaningful boundaries for the conversation. A guiding principle may come from scripture, from the mission of the organization, from its core values, or from its larger religious tradition. The chosen principles should feel important to the organizational body authorizing the discernment.[9]

The leaders at Stonecrest named the following guiding principles for their discernment:

As we consider our future in worship we will be guided by our commitment to:

• *Radical inclusivity,*
• *A reformed worship tradition,*
• *Excellence in the music and arts,*
• *A unified Sunday school hour.*

We will be open to alternative musical styles and levels of formality. We will embrace advances in technology.

When articulating the grounding principles, it is important to avoid contradictory statements or overly restrictive statements. Avoid letting personal agendas and biases creep into the guiding principles. If the group is having difficulty agreeing upon one or more guiding principles, it is generally helpful to step back, to simplify and broaden the principle(s), so everyone can buy in.

Shedding

Shedding involves naming and laying aside anything that might prevent the group from focusing on God's will as the ultimate outcome. Shedding invites participants to name and release unhelpful biases and ego investments in the outcomes. The process of shedding must be encouraged at both the individual and the group level. The process of shedding is invited when we say, "What needs to die in me/us for God's gifts and direction to find room in our lives?"[10]

Stonecrest leaders acknowledged their attachment to the congregation's reputation as the "biggest church in the region." They feared this ego attachment would block honest reflection on declining worship attendance. They also explored the congregation's reputation as the "best traditional worship experience around," recognizing it as a barrier to considering non-traditional forms of worship. Several members of the board acknowledged their personal investment in the choral ministry of the church, which might make them apprehensive and risk averse to considering changes in musical styles.

Shedding invites personal indifference. Discerners suspend personal preferences because they don't value anything as much as they value honoring the soul of the institution and knowing God's will. Indifference does not mean uncaring. During discernment, one remains deeply committed to the subject and cares about both the conversation and the outcome. One tries to be unconcerned about personal ego, the pride of the congregation, the politics of people involved, one's own comfort with the direction, or any personal advantage that may result from a shift in direction.

To invite shedding, I often distribute index cards and ask people to write down what they are certain they already know about the topic. Then I circulate an offering basket or plate through the room and invite each person to fold and place what they have written in the offering plate until our discernment is complete. In smaller groups, we may spend time openly confessing our attachments as a way of inviting accountability. Participants are welcome to pick up their card and resume their certainty once the process is finished. While the group is in discernment, the cards remain visible, a constant reminder of our commitment to remaining unattached.

The shedding process is never complete. We cannot fully and permanently eliminate our own ego bias. However, once group members have done their best to name and set aside their biases, the discernment process moves forward.

Listening

Listening involves attending to the voices and wisdom of people in the room, as well as other relevant constituents who are not in the room. Listening also involves waiting in stillness for Holy Spirit wisdom to manifest.

The listening phase of the discernment process can be as short as ten minutes in a single meeting, or it may last several months, depending on the discernment issue and the level of reflection warranted.

When a group determines that their listening needs to extend beyond the people in the room, they may employ multiple listening methods. Surveys, appreciative inquiry interviews, town hall meetings, and focus groups might be considered.

The discerning leaders at Stonecrest engaged in a listening process that spanned several months. They began by listening more deeply to one another. Then the discerners invited members of the staff team to join them in a dialogue about the joys, concerns, strengths, and weaknesses surrounding worship life at Stonecrest. Finally, the discerners created a congregation-wide listening process. They set aside several of the church's regularly scheduled Wednesday evening dinners for dialogue about the future of worship. They also facilitated several focus groups on Sunday afternoons to hear the views of those who could not attend a Wednesday evening session.

Listening also involves summarizing and interpreting what has been heard. If the listening phase of a discernment process is limited to a single session, the summarization is straightforward. One or two members of the group offer their observations about what has been shared and other members of the group affirm or amend those observations.

When the listening process has been lengthier, or when it has involved data gathering, the summarization and interpretation of what has been heard will be more complicated. Qualitative data gathering (interviews, focus groups, etc.) can generate copious notes that must be synthesized. Quantitative data gathering (demographic analysis, surveys, etc.) will generate metrics that must be analyzed.

When a discerning group is presented with data, particularly when the data is quantitative, the group may be lured into a decision-making stance. Data analysis moves us into left brain activity, which is logical and linear. When we are working from the left side of our brain, we are more inclined to debate and decide. It's fine for a discerning group to spend time in analysis, but the facilitator needs to draw the group back to its discerning stance— back into wondering about the data.

I find it helpful to remind groups that the answers to their questions don't lie in the data. The data help to inform the discernment, but at the end of the day the data will not tell leaders what to do. To symbolize this shift, after leaders have completed their analysis, I invite them to physically remove all reports, summaries, and survey results from our discernment space. I exhort them to trust that they have already learned what they need to know from the data. This creates an open space from which to continue the discernment process.

Exploring

The exploring stage of discernment is a comfortable stage for many groups, because it mirrors the brainstorming stage people are accustomed to in decision-making. In this stage, participants identify all possible directions or alternatives, evaluating each option, eliminating those that don't satisfy the guiding principles, until only two or three possible options remain.

The challenge in discernment is to narrow the options and yet avoid being captured by a single outcome while the exploration is still underway. The group works to make each option the best that it can possibly be. The group evaluates and improves upon each option without abandoning their indifference.

The leaders at Stonecrest Church identified three possible options for further consideration.

1. Keep the existing worship service but incorporate new technology and experiment with new musical styles.
2. Add an alternative worship service in Fellowship Hall at the same time as the existing worship service in the Sanctuary, embracing a different musical style and preaching format. Leave the existing worship experience largely untouched.
3. Invest in technology to broadcast the current worship experience to a broader audience.

Leaders determined that each of these three options were viable. Not all members of the group were equally excited about all options, but each member acknowledged some support for each option. The group felt that each option addressed the framing issue and honored the guiding principles.

Weighing

Continuing with the best two or three options, the group weighs each possibility. The group is asked to suspend its analysis of each option and to receive Spirit guidance. Having completed a vigorous analysis of possible alternatives, the group yields to intuition, insight, and wisdom.

A variety of discernment tools are available for helping a group weigh its options. A group might consider Biblical Theological Reflection. In this process, the group selects a biblical story that feels relevant to the discernment topic. They explore the ways in which the discernment issue is like or unlike the selected biblical story. They hold each possible option up for scrutiny by the characters in the passage, or they use a key lesson from the passage as an evaluative lens.

Alternatively, the group might use the Ignatian practice of consolation/ desolation. Sitting in prayer with each option, participants notice where they encounter the movements of consolation (feeling directed from beyond your-selves, being drawn into community, feeling inspiration, feeling restored, balanced, refreshed, led, energized). The group may also note the options that move them toward desolation (turning inward, being drawn toward negative feelings, feeling cut off from community, giving up on important values, feeling drained of energy).

There are a variety of group discernment tools available for weighing options. The facilitator must select an approach that feels most appropriate to the prayer practice and theology of the group.

Choosing

When the options have been weighed and the group seems ready to make a choice, the group facilitator might check for consensus. Consensuses looks for group solidarity in sentiment and belief. A consensus choice is not the same thing as a unanimous decision (in which all group members' personal preferences are satisfied). Consensus is also not a majority vote (in which some larger segment of the group gets to make the decision).

In consensus-based decision-making, the group works with an option until every person involved in the choice can say: "I believe this is the best decision we can arrive at for the organization at this time, and I will support its implementation." Simply agreeing or going along with a decision is not true consensus. Consensus implies commitment to the decision, which means that all participants oblige themselves to do their part in putting the decision into action.[11]

During a consensus check, as concerns are raised, it is the group's job to understand concerns before resolving them. The group listens carefully to each reservation raised, asking thoughtful questions to better understand the nature of the reservation. The group seeks or provides additional information to address the concern. Silence and prayer are used appropriately throughout to maintain detachment.

Any member of the group that continues to have reservations can ask to make his or her concern a point of record. This means that a public record is created (minutes) registering his or her reservation about the group's chosen course of action. The group might then ask the person with reservation if he or she would be willing to "stand aside" and allow the group to proceed, now that the concern has been registered.

When consensus is not possible because one or more members of the group don't feel that they can confirm the consensus or stand aside, the group has several options for continuing group discernment: [12]

1. Revisit the guiding principles and either reaffirm or reshape them. Then test again to see if new clarity around the guiding principles helped to resolve group differences.
2. Take more time for individual prayer and reflection. The additional time required may only be a matter of minutes, or it may take days/ weeks, depending on the issue and the available time frame. Many differences simply resolve with the passage of time or a shift in perspective brought about by prayer.
3. Decide by majority rule. If the need for a decision is immediate and consensus is still not clear, the group may decide to let the majority decide. This generally works best when a deadline for a decision has been set before the discernment: "If we are not at consensus by _____(date), we will decide by majority vote."
4. Drop the discernment. If the group decides that there is no clear leading in this matter, they may celebrate the process, claim what has been learned, and move forward with a fresh framing of a new discernment issue.

At Stonecrest, when the moment for choosing was at hand, each member of the discerning group was given a few minutes to share what they had experienced during the process. A scribe recorded the observations of each member. Then each member of the discerning team was asked to indicate which of the three options they could support and which options they could not faithfully consider. After forty-five minutes of shared reflection, consensus was becoming clear. It seemed that every member of the group felt energized by the option of adding an alternative worship service in Fellowship Hall at the same time as the existing worship service. A choice had been made.

Testing

There is one final step in the discernment process, a step rarely encountered in traditional decision-making. We test by resting. Before the decision is shared beyond the discerning group, the group is asked to sit with the decision in stillness and prayer. Sitting with the decision near to their hearts, we invite participants one last time to check for consolation and desolation. Ask, "Is our decision God's will, nothing more, nothing less, nothing else?" [13]

The group is reassembled and asked to share any insights from its time of rest. Each group member is consulted to determine if they are still able to support the decision moving forward.

A Lot of Work

A discernment process takes more time, energy, and intentionality than a decision-making process. Not all issues are significant enough to warrant this careful form of deliberation. However, when the issue is important or potentially polarizing, or requires significant buy-in, the process outlined here can be worth the investment.

Because the process is so time-consuming, many faithful organizations choose to blend discernment with decision-making. If we were to use a discernment process for every operational issue, the business of the church would likely grind to a halt. Or our pace of experimentation would be egregiously slow in an era when we need to learn and adapt quickly.

There are nuanced ways to blend decision-making and discernment. We may choose to do traditional decision-making, taking additional time during some parts of the process to work with discernment tools. Alternatively, we may design a discernment process that abbreviates a few of the steps to conform to the demands of a calendar.

A discernment process does not need to be long and laborious. A group can complete this entire process in a half-hour conversation during a regularly scheduled meeting. A discernment process can also be completed over the course of a weekend retreat, or over several months. The length of the discernment process depends upon the significance of the topic, the spiritual maturity of the leadership group, and the available time and energy of the discerning community.

WHERE IS THE CONVERSATION LOCATED?

The Stonecrest story illustrates how various groups can participate in a discernment process. The discernment process was shared by the board, the staff, the congregation, and a specially formed task force. The governing board framed the discernment topic at one of its regular board meetings. The board also named the guiding principles before turning the work over to a task force.

When it came time to listen to the voice of the congregation, the task force picked up the discernment. The task force conducted the survey and the focus groups. Task force members summarized and interpreted the data. Task force members began the exploration of options.

Next, the task force hosted a day-long retreat with the staff team and the board to complete the exploring, weighing, and choosing phases of the discernment. Leaders let the decision rest for a month after the retreat before the chosen option was brought before the board for approval. Board leaders tested their consensus at the next regularly scheduled board meeting and then called for a congregational vote to affirm their chosen path.

For a smaller discernment topic, the entire dialogue may be located within a single board or committee. For a larger discernment topic, phases of the discernment process may be assigned to different groups. A carefully designed process will elicit participation that is appropriate to the topic and context.

Who can ever fully know the mind of God? It is rare for a discerning group to receive an unambiguous message from the Holy Spirit, although that does occasionally happen. More often, a discerning group grapples with an interpretation of what is being called forth. With patience and attention, the discernment process ultimately elicits clarity, energy, and commitment among participants.

A community deepening its discernment practice is a community learning to get out of its own way. It is a community coming to understand that prayer is not simply a means of getting God to do what we want. Through prayer, stillness, and dialogue we place ourselves in alignment with God's purpose for us.

Learning to discern the movement of the Holy Spirit is life-changing for all who yield to the process. On a personal level, faith journeys are impacted in profound ways. People begin to value and trust their own ability to discern the mind of God in their personal lives. Collectively, the team is strengthened by their shared experience of having been led by the Holy Spirit. Humility, awe, and wonder permeate the life of a congregation that practices discernment.

NOTES

1. Ruth Haley Barton, *Pursuing God's Will Together: A Discernment Practice for Leadership Groups* (Downers Grove, IL: InterVarsity Press, 2012), 20.

2. Danny E. Morris and Charles M. Olsen, *Discerning God's Will Together: A Spiritual Practice for the Church* (Nashville, TN: Alban Books, by an arrangement with Upper Room Books, 1997), 18.

3. Morris and Olsen, *Discerning God's Will Together*, 26–37.

4. Victoria G. Curtiss, *Guidelines for Communal Discernment* (Louisville, KY: Presbyterian Church [USA]), 4.

5. These characteristics are adapted from Robert J. Sternberg, ed., *Wisdom: Its Nature, Origins, and Development* (Cambridge: University Press, 1990), 160–75.

6. Barton, *Pursuing God's Will Together*, 39.

7. Thomas H. Green, *Weeds Among the Wheat: Discernment—Where Prayer and Action Meet* (Notre Dame, IN: Ave Maria Press, 1984), 179.

8. Morris and Olsen, *Discerning God's Will Together*, 60.

9. Morris and Olsen, *Discerning God's Will Together*, 73–74.

10. Morris and Olsen, *Discerning God's Will Together*, 74–77.

11. Larry Dressler, *Consensus through Conversation: How to Achieve High-Commitment Decisions* (San Francisco, CA: Berrett-Koehler, 2006), 4.

12. Dressler, *Consensus through Conversation*, 35–40.

13. Morris and Olsen, *Discerning God's Will Together*, 90.

Chapter Five

Shaping Institutional Memory

Tell Me Our Story

God made man because he loved stories.
—Elie Wiesel

There are favorite family stories that my siblings and I love to retell. We recount these stories over and over, arguing over subtle nuances, celebrating our foibles and successes, and reflecting on lessons learned.

One favorite story is the legend of the broken crucifix. The crucifix hung in the hallway just outside of my parents' bedroom door. I imagine it was the same crucifix displayed in many Roman Catholic homes in the early 1960s. The metal crucifix was mounted on a wooden base shaped like a cross, with a secret compartment in which a small vial of holy water and two candles were stored. The secret compartment was covered with a dark glass plate. Jesus and the cross rested on this glass plate. The plate slid open to access the holy water and candles, in the event that anyone in the household needed the sacrament of *extreme unction*, the anointing of the sick.

I remember the crucifix as one of the most beautiful and sacred objects in our home. Every year on Palm Sunday we brought home a fresh palm frond, formed it into the shape of a cross, and tucked the palm behind the crucifix where it remained until the following Ash Wednesday. All the mundane actions that took place in our household over the course of the following year were sanctified by the daily presence of that cross.

One evening my parents went out and left my oldest brother in charge. He had just reached the respectable age at which he could be trusted with the well-being of his younger siblings. At first, the evening progressed in predictable fashion. We each tended to our own interests and my brother's "babysitting" skills remained unchallenged. At some point a skirmish broke out, over what I cannot recall. The sibling argument grew in intensity until a physical altercation between my two older brothers broke out. I eagerly joined in the fray. We started throwing things at one another and then it happened. Someone bounced into the wall and dislodged the crucifix.

My memory of the next moments takes place in slow motion. Three of us are standing and staring in horror at the wall as the crucifix slides downward. All three of us grab desperately at empty air but the cross slips through our outstretched fingers. The crucifix crashes to the floor, and the glass plate on which Jesus and the cross are mounted cracks in two. I am horrified that we have just committed some grave mortal sin, although which one I cannot say. Certainly, the breaking of the glass on which Jesus lay must be on par with the tearing of the curtain in the Holy of Holies, or the consuming of Sodom and Gomorrah by fire. We are doomed!

The fighting draws to an immediate halt. The intense skirmish so important moments before is completely forgotten. Our horror at our collective transgression and our conviction about the trouble we are in makes us fast allies. My oldest brother assesses the situation and takes charge. "We've got to get this thing fixed, now!" My second brother, the one who can fix anything, has a plan. He knows where Dad keeps the super glue and is certain he can mend the broken glass. I watch on in horror, whining about what is going to happen when Mom and Dad get home.

The repair seems to take hours, although in retrospect it is probably about fifteen minutes. My oldest brother rehangs the cross, but the break is clear to anyone who takes the time to really look. It seems to scream from the wall, "See me! I have been violated by these young ruffians!"

We work together to wash several scuff marks from the wall where the cross crashed into the baseboard. And then we swear an allegiance of silence. Both of my brothers are looking down on me and threatening me within an inch of my life if I squeal. We put ourselves to bed early, so no one will be awake when my parents return home.

The next days are agonizing for me. Each time that I pass the crucifix I glance upward, trembling under the broken countenance of Jesus. I surreptitiously sweep my glance from the crucifix to one of my brothers, whose immediate glare silences me, reminding me that I am dead meat if I say anything.

Remarkably, one day passes to the next and our transgression goes unnoticed. The uncelebrated victory is unsettling. Up until this moment I am convinced that my mother has eyes in the back of her head, and a remarkable capacity for detecting any misbehavior within a ten-mile radius of her. We never get away with anything. Yet remarkably, we seem to have gotten away with this. Mom never notices the cracked cross.

Until, that is, fifteen years later, when my parents are readying to sell the house. Most of us are home for the weekend, helping to pack things up and celebrate a life of memories in our childhood home. Mom takes the crucifix off the wall to wrap it for packing and says, "Wow. What happened here?" By now, the glue that held the cracked glass together has grown old and is discolored and crumbling. My siblings and I take one look at each other and burst into uproarious laughter as my perplexed mother stands in the center of our circle, Jesus clenched in her hand, looking from one of us to the next, awaiting the quieting of our laughter and an explanation.

What is it that makes this story so worth retelling in our family? We love remembering this incident as way of teaching ourselves some important truths. The story illustrates certain values that don't otherwise find easy expression.

First, this is a story that teaches about the value of sibling relationships. This was one of the first times we recognized our importance as an interdependent unit, separate from our parents. We could stick together, problem solve, and redeem one another through our mutual loyalty. We were important to one another and would go on to support each other in remarkable ways foreshadowed by this experience.

It is also a story about parenting. In the incident of the crucifix, we learned that our parents weren't all knowing and omnipresent. They were fallible human beings who might miss important details and be tricked like anyone else. That sobering realization aside, our parents also provided a home in which sacredness was emphasized, and they embraced rituals important enough to preserve and protect. They gave their children room to make mistakes and correct those mistakes without too much parental involvement.

Finally, it is a lesson about the forgiving nature of God. Over the years, gazing at the cracked glass beneath Jesus' crucified body became a physical reminder to me of God's abundant grace. This egregious act committed by my siblings and I was never fully repaired, but also never punished. The crucifix was broken. We were broken. It was all okay. Each day of my childhood that I passed by that broken cross reminded me of the wholeness that resides within brokenness.

When my siblings and I tell the story of the broken crucifix we do not stop to explain the lessons learned or the values emphasized. We simply tell the story. The story speaks for itself, and the interpretation of the story is left up to the hearer.

We each tell the story in a slightly different way. There is more than one version of the truth. For example, it is possible and truthful to tell this story without emphasizing the sacred nature of the crucifix. It's an honest telling to describe the cross as an artifact that was important to my mother, much like a favored lamp. That would be a factually correct story, but it would emphasize a different lesson. That telling of the story wouldn't have anything to do with God's grace but might illustrate children trying to protect their mother from the consequences of their recklessness. Or the story might emphasize the repercussions of secret keeping on relationships. There are easily a hundred truthful ways in which this story could be told and a variety of values that might be emphasized.

Remembering rightly is important work. The way in which we shape our memories and tell them from one generation to the next has powerful implications for identity, values clarification, and soul tending. This is true for individuals and institutions alike. How we remember shapes how we interpret our present circumstances, how we live into our values, how we make decisions, and how we claim our purpose. Memory work is soul-tending work.

REMEMBERING AS SACRED WORK

Aristotle said, "Memory is the scribe of the soul." We revere, venerate, and hallow our stories. This makes the work of remembering inherently sacred work. Our memories are not simply historical facts accumulated over time, or a recounting of our collective triumphs and tribulations. Our memories shape our identity. They are layered with interpretation and with the imposition of important values and beliefs. Our self-perception is as much about what we remember about our past as it is about any set of historical data about us. Similarly, the way that others perceive us is mostly based upon what they remember about us. Memory is central to self-awareness and other-awareness. Theologian Miroslav Volf reminds us that when we sever ourselves from memory, we lose our identity, particularly the part of our identity that is rooted in God.[1]

Jews and Christians are people of the Book. We are our biblical story, players in the unfolding drama that began within Adam and Eve. "Remember" is one of the most frequently used words in the Bible. Through scripture we are repeatedly encouraged to remember the story and to remember the love of God demonstrated through the story. "Remember the days of old, consider the years long past; ask your father, and he will inform you; your elders, and they will tell you" (Deut. 32:7). "Remember these things, O Jacob, and Israel, for you are my servant; I formed you, you are my servant; O Israel, you will not be forgotten by me" (Isaiah 44:21).

Furthermore, scripture tells us that our core identity is shaped by God's remembering of us and of his covenantal relationship with us.

> It shall come about, when I bring a cloud over the earth, that the bow will be seen in the cloud, and I will remember My covenant. . . . When the bow is in the cloud, then I will look upon it, to remember the everlasting covenant

between God and every living creature of all flesh that is on the earth. (Genesis 9:14–16)

He has remembered His covenant forever, the word which He commanded to a thousand generations. (Psalm 105:8)

Volf writes that to be a Jew is to remember the Exodus, and to be a Christian is to remember the death and resurrection of Christ. The purpose of the Passover Seder is not so much to convey historical information as it is to transmit a vital memory about the relationship between God and the Jewish nation. The Seder takes each participant back to Egypt, a hands-on reminiscence of captivity and redemption.[2]

Similarly, when Christians celebrate Holy Communion through scripture, liturgy, and song, they do not simply recall the Passion of Christ. Instead, they ritually narrate the death and resurrection of Christ as events in which they are personally implicated and redeemed. Volf says, "In remembering Christ, they remember themselves as part of a community of people who have died and risen together with Christ and whose core identity consists in this spiritual union with Christ. They remember Christ's story not just as his story but also as *their* story and the story of every human being."[3]

The sacred memories of both Jews and Christians are essentially communal memories. We remember our relationship to God as participants in a larger community that has passed the story from one generation to the next. Religious communities sustain sacred memories and find fresh and vibrant ways to transfer those memories to succeeding generations.

I believe that one of our agonies related to the current decline in organized religion is our fear that we are the weak link in the memory chain. We are the generation that may fail to pass the sacred stories forward. What if there isn't a next generation to whom we pass our story? Who, then, will we be? Volf reminds us, "Take the community away and sacred memory disappears; take the sacred memory away and the community disintegrates."[4]

Finally, the sacred nature of memory stems from its ability to shape our future. Our memories of the past ground our hope for the future. If our memories are rooted in experiences of reliability, trustworthiness, and love, we come to expect these same virtues in our future. The story of the Exodus tells not just of the deliverance that happened back then, but of the deliverance we expect in our own future. The resurrection of Christ didn't happen just to that first-century community; in remembering we know that it is happening now and that it will happen—again and again.[5]

REMEMBERING RIGHTLY

Revisiting institutional memories and tending to the ways in which we recount them is critical work in a liminal season. When we are between an ending and a new beginning, when we are neither here nor there, when we aren't certain what to do next, we turn to our memories to make meaning of our experience. Where have we come from? How did we get here? What then should we do next? Our memories serve as a touchstone, a benchmark for evaluating the authenticity of our available choices.

Volf writes about the challenge of remembering rightly. When we remember, we imagine that we are reciting facts, but we aren't. Our imagination has secretly come to the aid of our faltering memory, so we unwittingly pass fiction off as truth. We rely on memory to bridge the gap between our present and former selves. And memory is not necessarily trustworthy. The gap between now and then leaves space for falsehood to enter in, for imagination to supply whatever pieces memory is lacking. Most stories contain some measure of the truth but one that is independent of what happened. We tell ourselves a fictionalized truth. According to Volf, "The truth about the past is merely the story we find most compelling, either because it is attractive and useful to us or because it has been imposed upon us by some social constraint or subtle persuasion."[6] Consider the following Jewish fable as an illustration:

> A long time ago, there was a master archer who began to search the land for an archer of even greater talent so that he might study, learn, and improve his craft. After many months of walking through forests, meadows, and towns, he came upon a tree with an arrow in the exact middle of a painted target drawn on a tree. He became curious as he walked on and saw another tree with a perfectly centered bull's eye. Soon, he saw more and more trees that displayed straight arrows perfectly centered within the round targets. Perfect bull's-eyes peppered the forest. Suddenly, he entered a clearing and looked up and saw a barn with row after row after row of perfect bull's-eyes. He knew he had found his mentor. He began asking everyone he saw on the road, "Whose barn is it that displays so many perfectly centered arrows?" The people told him how to find the man who owned the barn. When he found this man he saw that he was a simple man, slow of speech, and seemingly awkward in his movements. Unperturbed, he asked the man to share his secrets. "How do you do it?" he asked. The man explained, "Anyone can. After I shoot the arrow, I take some paint and draw a target around the arrow."
>
> —A Jewish Teaching Story[7]

The stories that organizations tell about their past are all fictionalized accounts of some noteworthy experience. The accounts told are particularly complicated because they have been shaped over generations of telling and interpretation. The fiction we tell today is formed by the interpretation of facts that the original keepers of the story imposed upon it when they first told or recorded it. The fictionalized account is further shaped by the intervening generations as they have used the story, and finally by how we choose to tell the story today.

The work of the organizational leader is to help the institution examine its own memory and to reinterpret its core stories. The reinterpretation must honor the truthfulness of what happened (as best we are able to reconstruct that truth), and it must shape the telling of the memory in such a way that the values of the institution are elevated, introducing important new values as needed. An effective retelling of the memory helps an organization figure out what it needs to do next, based on the best of its past identity.

Anna's Story

There is a long-standing story told in a congregation I once called home. It is the story of Anna B. Quick, a laywoman who is credited with saving the church over one hundred years ago. She is the primary heroine of the congregation, and her portrait hangs in the church lobby to this day. Anna's story is one of the first stories that newcomers to the congregation are likely to hear and it is shared in new-member classes. Other stories are shared as well, largely about the contributions of previous male pastors, but Anna's story captures the imagination of this congregation. This is how the story is remembered.

As Anna's story begins, the congregation is dying; in fact, for all practical purposes it is dead. The building is run down and ill-suited for congregational life. The congregation can't afford to pay a minister, so there isn't one. Without a minister, people have stopped gathering for worship on Sunday mornings. However, Anna B. Quick shows up alone at the church every Sunday morning, week after week. She lights the lights and opens the doors just in case someone shows up for prayer. Anna files the annual papers that maintain the congregation as a legal entity. These simple acts of faithfulness keep the congregation alive for several years. The church barely survives this very difficult era, but eventually rebirth happens, and the congregation once again becomes a thriving community. All thanks to the diligence of Anna B. Quick.

That's the basic story. What values and life lessons is the congregation teaching itself when it repeats this story? It is a story of faithfulness, trust, and loyalty. Anna embodies all these virtues. And apparently God rewards Anna's faithfulness by revitalizing the congregation, or so we assume because the congregation survives for another one hundred years after Anna's story takes place. It is also an important story about the power of one individual, the voice of the laity, and the role of women in the church.

However, the story also embraces a troubling cluster of behaviors. Anna's heroism is attributed to the fact that she just keeps doing the same things that have always been done. She opens the doors, lights the lights, and files the reports. She doesn't change anything. She simply walks faithfully until the world rights itself again.

Fast forward one hundred years, and Anna's congregation is once again in trouble. Membership and attendance have declined so significantly that the congregation has let go of all staff, save their pastor. Most programming, including Sunday school, has disappeared, and the average congregant is more than sixty years of age. The new pastor of this congregation has been trying to introduce innovative ideas to the leaders. People verbally support his initiatives, but no one seems willing to invest time or energy in bringing new ideas to fruition. The congregation is stuck, but members still love to tell the story of Anna B. Quick, a story in which the heroine does nothing but the faithful few things that have always worked.

Out of curiosity and frustration, the pastor digs into the archives of the congregation to research the Anna B. Quick story. Remarkably, he learns fresh parts of the old story that the congregation never tells. It seems that revitalization of the old church happened when Anna and a few others gave sacrificially from their own personal income in order to hire a new pastor. Anna led the church in a decision to tear down the old building, and she helped raise the funds to build a new sanctuary. The church began to thrive once these bold initiatives were underway.

Why does the present-day congregation tell only a truncated version of the story when they remember Anna's role in the turnaround of the church? Because they want to believe that they can experience the same kind of revitalization with their simple acts of faithfulness and loyalty. They are frightened by the prospect of bold new initiatives and risky undertakings.

The part of the story that the congregation tells about Anna isn't false, but it isn't authentic to who Anna was. I am not certain at what point the Anna B. Quick story was truncated in its telling, but it is clear from the pastor's research that the congregation is not remembering rightly. The pastor began to teach Anna's more authentic story to the congregation as a way of introducing some risky changes on the horizon. He believed that the more authentic telling of Anna's heroism would draw the congregation out of its past and into the present by inviting members to play with new possibilities and embark on new paths inspired by Anna's courage. New values, important to the present and future of the church, were layered into the telling of the old story.

THE DANGER OF A SINGLE STORYLINE

Remembering rightly requires fulsome storytelling, memories that capture the complete messiness of all that may have transpired. Unfortunately, the memories that many of us pass along from one generation to the next are overly simplified and truncated. Single storylines that don't capture the full essence of all that came to pass.

Nigerian novelist Chimamanda Ngozi Adichie spoke at a TED Global conference in July of 2009. Her speech was entitled "The Danger of a Single Story."[8] Adichie spoke about the many overlapping stories that make up our lives. She warned that if we hear only a single rendition of a memory, event, or circumstance, we risk misunderstanding. We create stereotypes. We reduce complex people and events to a single knowable perspective to categorize and simplify our knowing. Adichie says, "Show a people as one thing, as only one thing, over and over again and that is what they become."

Adichie also says, "The shaping of memory is an exercise in power. Who determines what the predominant storyline is, who is allowed to tell it, which story becomes the definitive story?" People with power and in power are typically the ones allowed to shape the memories.

Adichie was speaking primarily about stories told in a cultural context, but her insights are also relevant in organizational settings. Events happen. There is no single truth about what has happened and no single memory that encapsulates the rich complexity of the institution in relationship to that event. People who were witness to a series of events each tell their rendition of what transpired. Over time, those multiple interpretations of what happened are told and reduced to a single, "tellable" story by those in power, and that story becomes part of institutional memory.

Some time ago I worked with a congregation that was preparing for pastoral transition. As part of their transition work, I invited them to "tell the stories" of previous pastoral transitions, in the hopes of surfacing values and lessons learned in times of leadership transition.

Storytelling began with the memory of a "successful" pastoral transition that had occurred twenty years earlier. Leaders told a succinct story of easy transition. In the telling of this story, leaders consistently recited the following phrase as they closed the story, "We've had only five senior ministers in our eighty-year history. We choose our pastors to last."

The problem with their tagline was that it ignored an important and real competing perspective, which we later uncovered through an interview with the senior pastor hired during that transition. He spoke of a prolonged period of mistrust on the part of leaders during which he had to prove himself time and again. The pastor described a tumultuous seven-year transition period before he was truly allowed to pick up the leadership mantle and shape the direction of the congregation. The downside of the long-tenured pastorates in this congregation was an organizational culture that was very resistant to change. This part of the collective story had not been incorporated into the single storyline of seamless successions.

In the same congregation, we continued our storytelling session by inviting leaders to tell the story of their most recent pastoral transition two years' prior, a transition that began with great hopes and dreams and that ended in failure. An identified candidate accepted the position but left the congregation within twelve months of the call. It wasn't easy to get at this story. Leaders had not given themselves permission to talk about the failed arrangement, because this was a congregation that did everything with excellence and had difficulty acknowledging failure. This failed chapter didn't support their tagline, "We choose our pastors to last." There wasn't yet a shared version of what had happened.

Some leaders attributed the failed transition to the problematic temperament of the incoming pastor. Secretly, some wondered if the ongoing presence of the exiting pastor had something to do with the failed transition, but no one felt that it was acceptable to suggest this out loud in a group. Several leaders approached me secretly behind the scenes to share this version of the story. It was clear that the developing narrative about the failed transition was being heavily shaped by those in power. The "in charge" group wanted a simple scapegoat story to tell. The problem was the incoming pastor. End of story. Those who carried conflicting memories weren't allowed to tell their story in a public setting.

Richard Hester and Kelli Walker-Jones write in their book *Know Your Story and Lead with It* about the use of narrative therapy techniques in leadership. The authors make an important distinction between thin and thick narratives. The teller of a memory gathers pieces of information and organizes them into a plotline that fits the teller's worldview. The teller of the tale "selects, rejects, connects, pares down, smooths out, and compresses a messy conglomeration of information to create a story of what has happened. And most of the information about the event remains on the cutting room floor."[9]

Hester and Walker-Jones explain that a narrative is thin when it contains minimal detail, reflects a narrow viewpoint, and fails to incorporate competing perspectives. A thin narrative will glide over ambiguity and conflict. It flattens the story down to an easily digestible sound bite, but it often leaves the hearer wondering, "So what? What was the point of sharing that particular memory?" In both these instances, where the congregation was asked to remember its previous pastoral transitions, the narratives shared were thin narratives. The storylines were underdeveloped, shallow, too easy to digest, and not particularly revealing about choices made or difficult waters navigated.

A thick narrative is one that presents a more comprehensive and richer storyline. It incorporates more detail. It reveals competing commitments and tension between values. It represents the viewpoints of multiple witnesses. In the Anna B. Quick case, the pastor took it upon himself to go back to the cutting room floor (i.e., the historical archives of the congregation) to find untold parts of the story. In doing so he thickened the narrative so that a richer set of circumstances and values were incorporated.

In a liminal season, when anxiety is high and uncertainty abounds, organizations are inclined to create thin narratives. To reduce anxiety, leaders compress memories to easily told tales that reassure and calm people down. Over time this results in impaired institutional memory. Our memories retain only the thin storyline.

In liminal seasons, organizations only have clarity about the past. The present is murky, and the future is unknowable. This condition can invite an unhealthy relationship with the past. We glamorize the past. We create thin narratives about how wonderful things were back then. Or we truncate our memories to block out experiences of pain and shame.

RESHAPING INSTITUTIONAL STORIES

The stories that congregations tell about their past are predictable: stories about the founding era, the glory eras, troubled chapters, hero figures, and lessons learned (who we are and how we got to be this way). Stories package the collective wisdom of the organization. The stories we tell symbolize our core values in action.[10]

Stories engage people deeply because they tell people what they already know, or already hope for. Stories also describe truths that may not be part of the collective consciousness of the organization.[11] We can raise the consciousness of an organization by asking leaders to reflect on their often-told stories.

Ask someone to tell a story, mirroring the way it is told in the organization. Once the story is told, ask people how the story makes them feel, and what the story makes them believe about the organization. What values, behaviors, and practices are reinforced when the story is told in this way? In what ways does the story empower or limit the choices before leaders today? What important facts may have been omitted over time? Whose side of the story is not represented in this telling?

Posing questions about the stories of an organization can help leaders realize that the stories do not represent objective truth. The stories can be reshaped to illustrate different truths or to reinforce alternate values.

Founding-Era Stories

Every organization has a founding story. Typically, a felt need became evident within a community. Or a group of people gathered around a shared skill set or passion. An experiment, program, or project was designed. That initial step was met with affirmation. Then the practical insight gained from the experiment was attached to resources and made available to others on a broader scale. An organization was born.

At some point in time, the facts behind the organization's birth become memorialized in story. Key characters are identified and imbued with heroic characteristics. A plot line is established that reveals the relationship between

the organization and its environment. An understanding of institutional vocation is incorporated into the storyline. "We were a pioneer church on the new
frontier." "Our founders brought these fundamental beliefs into the community." "We were the first organized church to reach out to the ____ people."

All organizations have a relationship with their founding story, even if the
present context is wildly changed and/or the mission is radically evolved.
There is something important about the values of the institution in the way
that it tells its founding story. "A concern for social justice and those who
live on the margins of society has always been a part of our story." "Providing a safe space to help families raise their children in faith has always been a
part of our DNA."

When the founding story is strong and positive, the role of the leader is to
shape the telling of the story in such a way that it has relevance for the
current chapter. The present-day story becomes an extension of the founding
story. "They did that—so we do this."

However, there are times when the founding story is lackluster, or even
problem saturated. "Our founding was the result of a church split, and we
have been a contentious congregation ever since." Or, "We were a new
church plant, mostly made up of people who were discontent with their old
congregations. Their discontent became part of our DNA. People are always
threatening to leave." Or, "It's generally well known that our founding members were also all members of the Ku Klux Klan."

When the founding story is problem saturated, it is the task of the leader
to shape a redeeming story. Organizations tend to bury their problem stories,
and the untold story infects the organization with shame. The presence of
shame in an organization is like a festering wound that does not heal. Story
has the power to clean the wound and promote healing. "Because we were
founded as the result of a church split, we have had to learn how to stay in
dialogue with one another through deep theological differences. Today, we
are known for the quality of our civil discourse." Or, "Our early congregational story is steeped in racism. To overcome the stigma of our past, we
have had to be intentional about issues of racial reconciliation." This refram-
ing of the founding story is truthful, but also points people toward a more
hope-filled future.

Hero Stories

Every organization has memories of heroes and heroines, people who modeled important values and behaviors during critical seasons of organizational
history. The Anna B. Quick illustration at the beginning of this chapter is an
example of a hero story. The facts related to the tale of the heroes are
generally recorded in some fashion in the historical documents of the congregation. How the hero story is memorialized changes from one season to the

next, depending upon the values that the organization currently finds important. The work of the leader is to listen to how the hero and heroine stories are being told and to authentically shape and thicken the story to support the important work that needs to be done in the current season.

Glory-Era Stories

"When were your glory days?" When I pose this question to congregational leaders, I almost always get a united response. Leaders may cite multiple eras in the organization's history, but in general the minds and hearts of leaders align around "who we were when we were at our best." For most organizations, the glory era was when attendance, participation, membership, and budgets were at an all-time high. The organization was growing in palpable and visible ways. Typically, the era is remembered in conjunction with a strong leader who is given credit for the thriving conditions.

Glory-era memories are almost always told as very happy stories. However, caution is required with these stories, because they almost always reflect some very limiting interpretation of success. There are a lot of positive emotions associated with glory era memories. "We were bursting at the seams." "Our classrooms couldn't hold all of the children that showed up on Sunday mornings." But glory-era stories are almost always thin stories that don't reflect a careful analysis of what accounted for success. They rarely recognize that in the midst of their success, bad seeds were sown that led to later downfall. They limit critical thinking about the present era, because they oversimplify life in the glory days.

The Trenton Church is a nationally recognized congregation in its tradition. The congregation's pulpit has long been regarded as home to the best and brightest in the denomination. The glory era of this congregation took place from 1993 to 2003, when a high-profile preacher occupied the pulpit. Energy was good, worship services were packed, and the congregation had plenty of resources to pursue ministry.

Ten years later the congregation is half the size that it was during its glory era. The current senior minister is respected as a strong administrator but isn't a particularly charismatic figure. She is a solid preacher but doesn't have the kind of status in the denomination that her predecessor had. The congregation seems to appreciate her leadership, but at times members question whether she is the right leader for this congregation. If only they had a preacher like _____, things could return to the way they were in the good old glory days of Trenton Church.

When the Trenton Church tells its glory day story, they emphasize the strength of the preaching and the energy and vibrancy of the senior minister. What the story doesn't reflect is the decline that began during that admired senior minister's tenure. He was a marvelous preacher. That part of the story is true. However, he was an awful administrator, and he built the success of the church on his personal persona. Programming was weak. The physical plant wasn't taken care of. The staff consisted of weak leaders in a poorly formed team. When the heroic senior minister took his leave, the place crumbled.

The congregation hired the current senior minister because of the administrative mess that was left in the wake of the glory-era minister's departure. This senior minister has the skills necessary to right the ship. However, the glory-era story doesn't buoy her leadership. It creates a gap between the idealized version of their past and the reality of what transpired. The glory-era story sets her up for unfair critique and comparison. "She'll never pack them in the way _____ did."

The glory-era story of this congregation sounds like a positive story because it feels happy in style and outcome, but it is a negative story, an unhelpful shaping of organizational memory. The people who hear the story walk away worse off for having heard it. The organization is damaged in some way by the telling and repeating of the story.[12]

The present leader's role in shaping this storyline is going to be tricky. She can't very well begin spreading stories about the incompetence of her predecessor. She can begin asking thoughtful questions about the congregation's story in the presence of her leaders. She can wonder about the story with them. "I wonder what values we are teaching ourselves when we talk about our high attendance era?" "What was limiting about that success?" "What kind of heroes will we need in our next chapter?" "How can we tell the stories of our past in ways that help the next generation of leaders to emerge?"

Who We Are Stories

Most organizations have stories that they tell themselves about why they work the way that they do, why they care about what they do, or where their problems stem from. These are "Who We Are" stories. Sometimes these are positive stories, in that they teach important values and move the organization in a healthy direction. At other times, these stories reinforce negative patterns of behavior and unhelpful stereotypes. They can hold an organization back during a liminal season when innovation and learning are important.

First Congregational Church has been struggling for years with insufficient finances to support congregation programs and staff salaries. Here is the story that they tell about the source of their problem:[13]

> Twelve years ago, we had a pastor who split our church. Thirty-five of our members went across town to start Cornerstone Church. That split really hurt

us in the long run. They got the moneyed members; we got the good real estate and the musical talent. We've been having financial problems ever since then.

Many people at First Congregational, even people who were not church members at the time of the "split," know and tell the story in exactly this way. The story appears in this form in the church's history archives. It has become part of congregational lore.

Notice how the congregation frames the story. It was a decision that was imposed upon them. They speak of this incident as a painful church split, which is typically language used to describe what happens when a faction of a church leaves during conflict.

Here's the rub. Cornerstone Church was not founded as the result of a split. It was a new church plant. The pastor, the one who has been vilified in the story, inspired thirty-five members to leave the safety of their prospering home church to move across town and open a new congregation in a rapidly growing part of the city.

The planted church, Cornerstone, is a thriving and vibrant faith community today. In fact, Cornerstone is doing better than its mother church. Instead of celebrating the role that First Congregational played in birthing a healthy community, leaders mourn the success of Cornerstone.

This story helps First Congregational explain its financial struggles, and it emphasizes its two best assets: location and music ministry. However, every time members retell this version of the story, they reinforce a scarcity mentality. They have shaped the story in such a way that they continually remind themselves, "Who we are is not enough." This story needs to be reshaped to invite a more hope-filled future.

Our Shameful Past Stories

Every organization has stories about its founding era and its glory days. Many organizations also have stories about a painful chapter that describes who they were when they were at their worst. These stories are almost always steeped in shame. Many times, there isn't even a coherent storyline, only a vague reference to a dark time, because the story is never openly talked about. When the story hasn't been told enough times, it hasn't yet coalesced into a meaningful narrative of the experience. The memory is swept under the rug as a denial of the past.

The pastor at Lord of Life abruptly resigns. He has been in treatment for depression and anxiety for some time. In the wake of his departure, leaders learn that the pastor has been having an affair with a member of the congregation. Then they learn that a series of affairs, many of which involved members of the congregation, have been taking place over the past fifteen years. Further investigation reveals that a member of the governing board had been providing the pastor with a regular place (the board member's condo) to host the illicit liaisons. The congregation is devastated.

When such an incident is raw and fresh, outside help is required to deal with the misconduct. I will not address here how the immediate situation ought to be handled, except to say that it needs to be managed with great care. Denominational support and legal help are needed. Policies need to be established, and careful work needs to be done to determine if other victims exist. Careful communication strategies need to be put in place.

However, as the years pass, and the situation becomes a more distant memory, shaping a cogent story can facilitate congregational healing. The longer the story goes untold, the deeper the shame becomes. The more repressed the shame, the unhealthier the organization grows. To heal a spiritual or psychological wound, the wounding event must be remembered, and it must be remembered rightly. According to Miroslav Volf, the rightful remembering of a painful past event must incorporate these elements: [14]

1. *Remembering as truthfully as possible.* It is never possible to reconstruct an objective truth, because so many variations of the story exist. However, for healing purposes, it is important to recount as factual of a memory as possible from the reconstructed data. Untruthful memories are unjust memories.
2. *Acknowledging the wrong that was done.* If the wrongdoing is not remembered, if it is never publicly named, it remains invisible. Volf says, "Its victim is not a victim and its perpetrator is not a perpetrator: both are misperceived because the suffering of the one and the violence of the other go unseen. A double injustice occurs—the first when the original deed is done and the second when it disappears."
3. *Viewing the remembered experience in a new light.* When we look back on the past event, we tell how the story has led to healing and redemption. Perhaps we tell of the ways we have all learned to function with better boundaries, how careful we were with the story of the victims, how we dealt with our shame and grew through the experience, how God's grace and mercy became palpable to all of us as a result of the ordeal.
4. *Protecting victims from further suffering and violence.* The shaping of the memory cannot cause any further suffering for possible victims. The confidentiality of victim identity must be maintained unless the victim has asked to be named. In shaping the memory, the leader must take care that additional unknown victims are not harmed in the telling.

Shaping a story that satisfies all these criteria sometimes feels downright impossible. But it is worthy work that justifies the struggle. When an organization is bound by the shame of an untold story, God's grace has no place to break through. We must learn to speak the truth about our unstoried memories.

Shaping Emergent Stories

Remembering rightly also involves listening for the story that an organization is telling about its present experience, the way it is shaping its future memories. The leader listens to how people tell the story of their own involvement with the organization, how they answer the questions, "Who am I? Why am I here? What are my hopes for the future?" Then the leader begins to frame a collective narrative that is truthful, value-laden, and hopefilled. She elevates present-day heroes and heroines. She emphasizes core values important to the current era of organizational leadership. She connects her story with the story of the organization. She connects the present-day experience of the congregation to its historical past and its place in the larger biblical story.

Shaping the organization's emergent experience begins with listening. When leaders make space to listen to the stories of their constituents, they cultivate collective wisdom. Story listening communicates respect and creates a bond between the storyteller and the listener. To receive the story of another is to bear witness to his or her experience. It is a sacred act. Telling and receiving stories breaks through illusions of separateness and activates a deep sense of our collective interdependence and the bonds that form us as community. When I tell you who I am and what is important to me about being here, I invite you into my journey and vice versa.[15]

The Church on Main Street was looking to develop deeper bonds of friendship within the church and to foster connected community. Leaders introduced faith-based storytelling as a practice in all board meetings, committee meetings, and educational venues. For a period of one year they adopted this discipline: ten minutes were reserved at the beginning of each meeting for someone to share a personal testimony or a personal story of faith. Over the course of the year, leaders found their relationships with one another deepening and they sensed greater clarity about the congregation's identity. Many of the stories that had been shared throughout the year illustrated the congregation's role in healing and recovery: from physical and emotional trauma, and from addiction. The distinctiveness of the congregation was emerging as a place of unconditional acceptance, healing, and hope.

At the end of one year, leaders decided to extend their storytelling practice indefinitely. Church leaders discovered that through storytelling they were shaping a meaningful collective narrative and deepening their sense of connection.

Using Appreciative Inquiry

In an organizational setting, an effective tool for storytelling and listening is Appreciative Inquiry (AI). In AI leaders invite constituents to tell stories of their peak experiences in the organization. Participants are invited to reflect on who the organization is when at its best. Leaders use those positive stories to claim common themes and to identify the root causes of past success. Building on this positive core, the organization shares its hopes and dreams for an emerging future.

AI begins with the assumption that every organization has some things that work very well—things that give the organization life when it is most alive, effective, successful, and connected in healthy ways to both its constituents and community. These strengths can be the starting point for creating positive momentum and lasting change. Furthermore, AI asserts that the very language we use to talk about our experience matters. When we focus on our best experiences, we create positive energy that draws the organization forward. Positive language inspires positive commitment and invites transformation.[16]

AI understands that people have more confidence in their journey into an unknown future when they carry forward meaningful parts of their past. This is what makes AI an effective leadership tool in a liminal season. Confidence and trust can be built into an organization that is in liminal space by creating direct links between stories of the past, present, and unknown future. Describing the best parts of our past helps us articulate those critical strengths that will protect us as we move into our future.

Pastor Karen entered her new pastoral assignment thoughtfully. She was intentional about discovering the narrative of the congregation. What stories did they tell about their past? How did people connect their story with the story of the congregation? What were their hopes and dreams for the future of the congregation? Toward this end, Karen scheduled a series of house meetings with her new parishioners. Each meeting included between twelve and eighteen participants. Each person in attendance was paired with a partner, and the partners recorded one another's responses to the following six appreciative-based questions:[17]

1. Reflecting on your entire experience at our church, remember a time when you felt the most engaged, alive, and motivated. Who was involved? What did you do? How did it feel? What happened as a result?
2. What are the most important contributions the church has made to your life? Tell me when this happened. Who made a difference? How did it affect you?

3. Don't be humble; this is important information: Tell me about a time when you made an important contribution to our church—through your personality, your perspectives, your skills, your activities, your character? What was happening? Who else was involved? How did you make a difference?
4. Tell me about an important spiritual experience, growth in belief, or step of faith that has occurred for you in this congregation. Describe what, when, how, and where this happened.
5. What are the essential, central characteristics or ways of life that make our church unique?
6. Make three wishes for the future of our congregation? Describe what the church would look like as these wishes come true.

Pastor Karen facilitated twenty of these house gatherings during her first six months as the new pastor. She ended up with stories and impressions from three hundred congregants. By the end of the process she had established herself as a credible witness to the stories of the congregation. People felt listened to and understood, and Karen had accumulated meaningful data that guided the first three years of her leadership.

Karen learned that this congregation prided itself on the quality of their civil discourse around politically contentious issues, the excellence with which they incorporated music and the arts into worship, the effectiveness of their children's program, and the beauty of their campus. She also documented a shared sense of hope about revitalizing youth ministry, reducing the level of debt, and hopes for better partnerships with community organizations.

By listening to personal stories of engagement with the congregation, Karen was able to shape a unifying narrative. While this congregation stood between an old era of leadership and a new chapter not yet apparent, Karen was able to build a powerful narrative about the distinctiveness of the past and some shared hopes for the future.

Finding the story and living the story is critical work for a liminal season. In this chapter, we have outlined various forms of storytelling work that nurture the soul of the institution. We can mine the stories that an organization tells to learn more about the strengths and limitations of its past. We can reshape some of those memories to tell better stories, stories that leave the hearer and the institution between equipped to face into its future. We can listen for the stories that are emerging now, and we can shape more intentional narratives that create a positive hope-filled future.

Most importantly, we can listen to the individual stories of our constituents, helping to connect their stories in meaningful ways. We can inspire confidence in our own leadership by connecting our story with the story of the organization, and by connecting the story of the organization with the biblical story. In this manner, we create meaning in the midst of a confusing chapter and negotiate a pathway through liminality.

NOTES

1. Miroslav Volf, *The End of Memory: Remembering Rightly in a Violent World* (Grand Rapids, MI: Eerdmans Publishing Company, 2006), 24–25.

2. Volf, *The End of Memory*, 96.

3. Volf, *The End of Memory*, 98–99.

4. Volf, *The End of Memory*, 100.

5. Volf, *The End of Memory*, 101.

6. Volf, *The End of Memory*, 47.

7. Annette Simmons, *The Story Factor: Inspiration, Influence, and Persuasion Through the Art of Storytelling* (New York: Perseus Books, 2009), 83–84.

8. Chimamanda Adichie, "The Danger of a Single Story," Online video clip. TEDTalks. Recorded July 2009. Viewed September 7, 2016.

9. Richard L. Hester and Kelli Walker-Jones, *Know Your Story and Lead with It: The Power of Narrative in Clergy Leadership* (Herndon, VA: The Alban Institute, 2009), 11.

10. Peg C. Neuhauser, *Corporate Legends and Lore: The Power of Storytelling as a Management Tool* (Austin, TX: PCN Associates, 1993), 29.

11. Gil Rendle, "Narrative Leadership and Renewed Congregational Identity," in *Finding Our Story: Narrative Leadership and Congregational Change*, edited by Larry A. Golemon (Herndon, VA: Alban Books, 2010), 24–26.

12. Neuhauser, *Corporate Legends and Lore*, 11–13.

13. This story, written by Susan Beaumont, originally appeared in "Giants and Grasshoppers: Stories that Frame Congregational Anxiety," a chapter in *Finding Our Story*.

14. Volf, *The End of Memory*, 27–33.

15. Simmons, *The Story Factor*, 186–92.

16. David Cooperrider, Diana Whitney, and Jacqueline Stavos, *Appreciative Inquiry Handbook: The First in a Series of AI Workbooks for Leaders of Change* (San Francisco, CA: Berrett-Koehler Publishers, Inc., 2005), 3.

17. These questions are adapted from Mark Lau Branson, *Memories, Hopes, and Conversations: Appreciative Inquiry, Missional Engagement, and Congregational Change* (Lanham, MD: Rowman & Littlefield Publishing Group, Inc., 2016), 76.

Chapter Six

Clarifying Purpose

Who Do We Choose to Be?

We have within us a compass pointing to the magnetic north of God.
—Cynthia Bourgeault

Humans cannot live without meaning. The greater our sense of uncertainty, the more desperately we grasp for a handhold, a shred of something purposeful that reminds us of who we are and what we are meant to do.

In the heart of a liminal season, when something has ended and we don't know where we are headed, people need help interpreting their past. People also need to know that they are pursuing something that matters now: worthy work, a shared common cause, or a sense of rootedness to something enduring. Thomas Merton said, "Humans have a responsibility to find themselves where they are, in their own proper time and place, in the history to which they belong and to which they must inevitably contribute."[1]

In the absence of meaning and purpose, people become fearful. Fearful people will attach themselves to anyone who promises to reduce their anxiety. Often, this involves attachment to one who promises a return to the past—a promise to restore the glory days of the institution, without thinking critically about the ills of that era. Unhelpful attachments to the past do not serve an organization well. These attachments merely deny the conditions that gave birth to liminality and they prolong disorientation.

Meaning and purpose are two closely related but distinct concepts. Meaning making is past oriented. It relates to something that has already been accomplished. In meaning making we examine what has happened and connect it to our highest values. We did *this* in service to *that*. "Our members gave sacrificially so that we could build this magnificent sanctuary, to the glory of God and for the benefit of future generations." Meaning making also addresses the shortcomings and foibles of our past. "Our commitment to this building has saddled us with ongoing debt and restricts some of our options in ministry."

Purpose clarification is present and future oriented. It is action based. Our purpose clarifies how we intend to make a difference and be useful in the world moving forward. How will we create something of value now? For example, "We are rediscovering the community around our building at the intersection of First and Main Streets. We are committed to serving the people who call this community home today."

During more stable times, organizations use strategic planning to create shared meaning and to clarify purpose. In traditional strategic planning, we develop shared perspective about our history as well as consensus about the mission and vision of the organization. We declare breakthrough objectives that describe our next areas of growth. We create action plans for achieving those objectives. We build shared momentum.

Strategic planning is *not* the best way to clarify purpose during a liminal season. Traditional strategic planning makes linear assumptions about how the future will unfold. We are standing here, and we want to get there. These incremental steps will take us there. In liminal seasons learning and logic are not linear. We build the bridge as we walk on it. Carefully crafted plans may inhibit the journey by locking us into decision-making rather than letting us discern our way to the other side.

Planning doesn't serve us well in liminality, but we don't have to wander aimlessly. We can gain clarity about who we are now: our passions, our giftedness, and our yearnings. We have some sense of who we are meant to serve, although this part of our identity may be shifting. We can clarify what we stand for, a set of core values that describe our fundamental beliefs and guiding principles. We have a sense about what we are trying to learn. And we can claim the next step in the general direction of our aspirations. Leaders can help an organization clarify each of these component parts of their purpose.

WHO ARE WE? (EXPLORING IDENTITY)

When the identity of an organization is in flux, some parts of the old identity have died. New passions and skills are emerging. Leaders must attend to these shifts, naming what has ended, clarifying what is arising, resourcing what seems to be emerging.

Something new is arising in the identity of Broadstreet Church. Several years ago, a few new families began attending worship. These families each had a child with special needs. Simultaneously, the congregation was approached by a non-profit organization seeking rental space. The non-profit uses creative arts to develop the potential of cognitively impaired children. Leaders attended to this synchronicity. They welcomed the non-profit and began channeling church resources into inclusive education and programming. This intentionality attracted more families with kids with special abilities and needs, which in turn attracted additional resources.

Within a few years, Broadstreet became known for its commitment to all-abilities inclusion. Today, the staff team includes professionals with training in education and pastoral care for those with special needs. Religious education curriculum has become multi-sensory and individualized, based on parent input and staff recommendations. Many volunteers have been trained to provide support to students with special needs. Worship accommodates the needs of those who are deaf and blind. Ushers provide hearing protection for children with autism who are particularly sensitive to loud sounds. A new "no-shush" worship service has been added for families whose members don't feel comfortable in the quieter confines of a traditional worship experience.

Not every member of the congregation participates in the all-abilities inclusion ministry. The church offers many ministry opportunities that aren't specifically related to kids and adults with special needs. However, inclusion has become a core piece of this congregation's identity. The shift in congregational identity at Broadstreet would not have happened if leaders hadn't attended to what was arising: a few new families with unique gifts and needs, coupled with a new tenant that contributed special skills.

Discovering a New Identity

Congregational identities often stagnate. We assume that who we are today is who we have always been. Perhaps we see ourselves as a loving, caring community that helps families raise children in our faith tradition. But then we look around and realize that we no longer have families with young children. Somewhere on the journey, we stopped attending to how our identity was shifting.

St. Mark's averages thirty-five people in worship attendance. The congregation has been in decline for many years, largely due to changing demographics in the community. The neighborhood surrounding the church is now predominantly Muslim. In recent years, the church tried introducing programs geared to Christian families with young children. Most of these programs failed from lack of participants. Now, leaders have given up on trying anything new, believing that a Christian congregation in a Muslim community can't possibly thrive.

The pastor of St. Mark's belongs to a local clergy support group that includes community pastors, rabbis, and imams. The clergy group is looking for a host organization to sponsor interfaith dialogue in response to anti-Jewish and anti-Muslim sentiment in the region. For a variety of reasons, St. Mark's turns out to be the ideal location. St. Mark's members rally to support the interfaith dialogue. Volunteers provide meals and ensure that the building is clean and welcoming.

After the dialogue, members decide it is time to embrace their identity as a minority organization in a multi-cultural community. They look for ways to serve their Muslim neighbors and to educate people in the community about the richness of multi-cultural interaction. They open their sanctuary to outside speakers and work to promote attendance at those events.

In time, St. Mark's begins to attract new members who are also interested in multi-cultural dialogue. Regrettably, the congregation loses some long-tenured members who don't like the new focus and are resentful about Muslim migration into their community. Those losses are painful to the members who remain. However, the congregation continues to nurture its new identity. Members feel more alive in their faith than they have for many years.

Leading a congregation whose identity is shifting is difficult work. The process is an exercise in attending and surrendering. We begin by naming the old identity, the identity to which we have been clinging. We acknowledge all the important ways that our old identity has served us well in our past. We surrender the loss of that identity, without fully knowing what will replace it. We cope with the accompanying grief and anger attached to our loss. We attend to what is emerging as we walk forward in faith, trusting that a new identity is unfolding.

In the movie *Indiana Jones and the Last Crusade*, Jones comes to the edge of precipice overlooking a huge abyss, with no apparent way to cross to the other side. He is chased by his enemies, and he must cross over to save himself and his dying father. A map in Jones' possession assures him that a bridge exists, but Jones can't see the bridge. He has no choice but to take a single step, a leap of faith, trusting that the bridge is there and will support his weight. He takes one frighteningly bold step forward and the bridge magically materializes. It was there all along, but Jones couldn't see it from his vantage point.

Nurturing a new congregational identity requires a similar leap of faith. We step out with confidence, trusting that a new identity awaits us, once we are ready to engage it. A congregation can't plan a new identity from the safety of the boardroom. Leaders can't cling to an old identity while systematically planning new pathways. We must trust that something important will be given to us that is worth the risk of letting go.[2]

Otto Scharmer, author and professor of management at the Massachusetts Institute of Technology, refers to this process as "letting go and letting come." Something happens that shifts our habitual way of seeing things. We let go of what no longer serves us. We listen to what is emerging from within ourselves: deeper intentions and new aspirations. We engage a new way of being in relationship to the world.

Scharmer compares this process to threading the eye of a needle. He reminds us of what Jesus said, "it is easier for a camel to go through the eye of a needle than for a rich man to enter the kingdom of God" (Matthew 19:24). In ancient Jerusalem there was a gate called "the needle," which was so narrow that when a fully loaded camel approached it, the camel driver had to stop and take off all the bundles so that the camel could pass through. Likewise, to discover an emerging identity, a congregation must shed what is non-essential. After crossing the threshold, we are pulled forward and up-ward into a space of new possibility. [3]

WHO DO WE SERVE? (EXPLORING CONTEXT)

In asking ourselves the question, "Who do we serve?" we are locating our-selves in time and place. What is most appropriate to this historical moment and the particularity of this place? Our congregations don't live abstractly on some aspirational plane. They are rooted in communities with unique demo-graphics and real needs.

In the tenth chapter of the Gospel of Luke, Jesus is speaking to a group of followers when an expert in the law stands and poses a question meant to challenge Jesus. "Teacher," he asked, "what must I do to inherit eternal life?"

"What is written in the Law?" Jesus replies. "How do you read it?"

The challenger answers, "'Love the Lord your God with all your heart and with all your soul and with all your strength and with all your mind'; and, 'Love your neighbor as yourself.'"

"You have answered correctly," Jesus replies. "Do this and you will live."

But the challenger wants to justify himself, so he asks Jesus, "And who is my neighbor?"

In response to this second question, Jesus goes on to share the parable of the good Samaritan.

Who is our neighbor? Certainly, our definition would include the people who show up on our doorstep, those who include themselves in the life of our congregation. But there are other ways that we define our neighborhood: the neighborhood surrounding our building, the neighborhoods in which our constituents live and work, the neighborhoods that we travel to in our mis-sion and outreach work. These geographies may overlap, but they may also be quite distinct.

For many years, local congregations didn't have to grapple with this question. We served everyone who found their way to us. Most of those people were from the neighborhood within a five-mile radius around the church building. Our constituencies tended to be very homogenous. We only

engaged people on the other side of the city, nation, or world through ministry coordinated by our denominational agencies.

Today, context is less bound by geography. We are more regionally and
globally connected. People will travel great distances to find a congregation
that is to their liking. Some congregations forge relationships with communities on the other side of the world, without the help of denominational
agencies. Many congregations offer online opportunities for worship and
study, so constituents may have little attachment to the physical properties of
the church. We may know nothing about the identity or demographics of
these virtual attenders who think of themselves as part of our congregation.

These fundamental shifts are causing some congregations to mistakenly
think that they serve the world. They seek to be all things to all people so that
no one feels excluded. In fact, a congregation who believes it is serving the
world, the nation, the denomination, or even the city in which it resides is a
congregation without clarity of purpose. Clarity of purpose requires narrowing in on context. We don't have unlimited resources. We cannot be all
things to all people. So who is our neighbor?

I learned an important lesson about clarity of context during seminary,
when I had the opportunity to work on the staff of a mega-church for one
year. Kensington Community Church was a seeker-sensitive church with a
weekend worshipping community that averaged five thousand. Today, this
congregation worships on eight campuses with over twelve thousand in
weekly attendance. From Kensington, I learned the value of understanding
context and narrowing focus. Leaders at Kensington were crystal clear about
who they were serving and the difference they were called to make in the
lives of those they served. I believe that their clarity accounts for at least
some of their exponential growth.

The mission statement of Kensington Community Church at that time
was "To reach those who feel God is irrelevant and transform them into fully
devoted followers of Jesus Christ." Leaders also had a much more specific
understanding of who they were called to serve. "We are called to reach the
unchurched thirty-five-year-old male." This contextual statement was not
listed on the website or printed in the public documents of the congregation.
However, this focus was ingrained in every meeting I attended during my
tenure. In worship planning, when decisions were being made about song
choice or worship themes, someone would ask, "What does the unchurched
thirty-five-year-old male want to hear?" The question was posed again when
selecting a fundraising strategy or determining a small-group approach. This
focus infused every major and minor leadership choice of the church.

Why the unchurched thirty-five-year-old male? When the founding pastors studied the community targeted for their church plant, they discovered
that young, newly married men were not attending church—anywhere. Furthermore, the founding pastors knew how to speak the language of this

demographic group. The three founding pastors were males in their early forties, raising families of their own. They yearned to reach this underrepresented demographic for the church.

Frederick Buechner said, "The place God calls you to is the place where your deep gladness and the world's deep hunger meet."[4] The founding pastors at Kensington found the intersection of their deep gladness and a long unaddressed hunger in their community. They were clear about who they were called to serve.

This focus may seem overly narrow, particularly given the size of the congregation. However, it had broad and lasting impact. Kensington created one of the finest children's ministries anywhere around. Why? Because thirty-five-year-old males are not going to attend a church unless their children are eager to attend. Similarly, Kensington had the finest women's ministry in town, even though no one on staff was assigned to support a women's program. How did such an outstanding women's ministry emerge in a church that was focused on men? Because women were willing to invest significant volunteer hours to build the program that they wanted, simply to be in a congregation where their husbands felt engaged.

Now, some of you may find this male focus off-putting, an example of patriarchy run amok. It may not be at all appropriate for your congregational context. But it was appropriate for Kensington in that era, and I believe it accounts for a great deal of the congregation's impact and growth. It is worth noting that this is no longer the primary focus of the congregation. The congregation's context is different today, and so is their understanding of who they serve.

Most mainline Protestant congregations are not able to get quite this clear about who they serve. Kensington was only nine years old at the time I worked with them and the founding pastors were still on staff. Congregations with a long history, who have been through many pastoral transitions, will include complex groups with competing needs. Nevertheless, clarifying context is fruitful work for a congregation, particularly during a liminal season. Who do we feel called to serve, today?

In the sixth chapter of the Book of Acts we read about the selection of the first group of deacons in the church, "seven men of good standing, full of the Spirit and of wisdom," who were appointed to the task of food distribution. The seven specifically included some Hellenists who were selected because of their ethnicity. The Hellenist widows had been neglected in the daily distribution of the food. Here we have it. An early community gaining clarity about context and deciding who they were called to serve with the resources available to them.

An organization seeking clarity of context is likely to encounter resistance from those who don't like the distinctions chosen. "If you are going to be about that, then what about me?" Gaining clarity about who we serve doesn't have to result in the exclusion of others who are not in the target group. As the Kensington example illustrates, many groups beyond the target group benefit from the energy that comes with clarity. Someone who doesn't fit our target description of "neighbor" doesn't need to feel excluded from our ministry to that neighbor. Everyone is invited to serve.

At the same time, should someone feel that the congregation's calling doesn't align with their personal passion and energies, we should not go to extraordinary efforts to keep them with us. We should bless them and support them as they find a place to serve that is more suited to their personal vocation.

WHAT DO WE STAND FOR? (EXPLORING VALUES)

Today, we use the term "touchstone" to refer to a benchmark or standard of comparison. An athlete's outstanding performance at an event becomes a touchstone against which they measure every subsequent effort.

Historically, the term touchstone referred to a physical stone that was used for assaying precious metals, for determining the purity of an alloy. The touchstone was a small tablet of dark stone such as fieldstone, or slate. The stone had a finely grained surface, so that a soft metal rubbed against it would leave a visible trace. A pure piece of silver would produce a recognizable color. Another alloy rubbed alongside the silver mark would leave a different colored trace. A merchant could compare the two colors to determine the purity of a piece of metal being offered for trade.

An organization in a liminal season needs a touchstone, metaphorically speaking. When everything in the environment is in flux, something standard and predictable is needed to evaluate the worthiness of choices.

In the very broadest sense, the mission of the organization is an important touchstone. Mission statements tell us why an organization exists. However, mission statements are not specific enough to ground discernment or decision-making. For example, a United Methodist congregation exists to make disciples of Jesus Christ for the transformation of the world. This is an important directional statement. However, it offers little guidance to a congregation that must discern whether to partner with a local warming shelter, a shelter that only works with constituents who are sober and employable. The warming shelter certainly supports the mission of the church, but the operating principles of this shelter may not resonate with the truest self of this congregation. Is the shelter a good investment of the limited resources for this congregation in this season? Something more is needed to ground discernment. Core values can serve this purpose.

Core values are the principles and beliefs that define who we are when we are operating as our best selves. Core values have an aspirational quality about them, but they are also grounded in real experience. Values are not just "pie in the sky" statements that describe any good congregation. They are true to the historical experience of this congregation. When we are at our best, we embody these principles.

Core values are not descriptions of our mission, the work we do, or the strategies we employ. They are not things we do; they are principles we hold and beliefs we share. Well-written values reflect the distinctiveness of an organization. An outsider reading an organization's value statement ought to be able to intuit attributes of the organization from what he or she is reading.

Organizations have an entire universe of values that they may draw upon (fairness, truthfulness, compassion, empathy, kindness, justice, etc.). However, the core values are those central tenets that are so primary, so central to the life of the congregation, that they remain stable through changes in leadership and shifts in the environment. The enduring nature of core values makes them useful as touchstones in decision-making and discernment.

This is not to say that core values are static. From one era to the next, subtle shifts in core values occur, sometimes producing remarkable changes over long stretches of time. The values that guide a congregation in its founding era may be quite different from the values that ground the same congregation fifty years later. However, these shifts tend to occur gradually.

The following core values were written by the leaders of United Church. Notice the aspirational nature of the values, what the congregation believes about its work in the world, and how they approach their work. What conclusions can you draw about this congregation when you read their values statement?

Every Person Matters: Each person is created in the image of God, endowed with creativity and entrusted with spiritual gifts. We are each called to make a unique and humble contribution to the world.

Taking the Next Step: Discipleship is a journey, an ongoing pilgrimage that begins where we are. We are guided in each stage of the journey by engagement with Scripture and the Holy Spirit.

Authentic Community: We are better together than we are alone. We seek to be a community that God might dwell among—loving, open, truthful, welcoming, and non-judgmental.

All of Life Is Worship: God is good. We respond to God's goodness with reverence and praise. Opportunities for worship exist in every aspect of our lives: in work, play, study, prayer, giving, and service.

Love in Action: God loves people, and so we love people. We show God's love to the world through action born of compassion. Avoiding judgment, we seek to embody the love of Jesus Christ through tangible acts of service.

Sending Out: God told us to spread the good news of the Gospel. We send empowered and equipped disciples of Jesus Christ into the world. Every member of our community is a missionary every day.

Clarifying Core Values

If core values are going to be useful, then they must be rooted in the lived experience of the organization. We cannot simply create a wish list of how we would like to be seen by the world. We must describe what we are actively trying to embody, who we are when we are at our very best. This means that core values must be socially validated—drawn from the experience of the organization and affirmed by its constituents.[5]

There are a variety of ways for an organization to socially validate its core values. One approach is through storytelling. Using the principles of Appreciative Inquiry, a group of constituents from the organization gather to tell stories about their peak experiences in the organization. "Tell me a story about a time when you felt most proud of being part of this congregation. What was happening? Who was involved? What did those positive feelings prompt you to do?" or "Reflecting on your entire experience at (name of the organization), remember a time when you felt the most engaged, alive and motivated. Who was involved? What did you do? How did it feel?"

Participants gather to tell their stories, first in small groups and then in a larger group. The exercise begins in groups of six. Small group participants listen to the stories of one another and then reflect on the core values common in the stories that were shared. Each small group distills their observations down to five value statements. Then the small groups report out to the larger group and the larger group looks for congruent themes.

Another approach is to clarify core values after doing a history review of the congregation. Constituents create a decade-by-decade record of the prouds and sorries of the congregation. They record important events, milestones, and key players from each era of the organization's history.[6] Once the story of the organization has been told, participants are invited to name the enduring principles and beliefs that have guided the organization across time.

Finally, core values can be clarified by examining the more recent decision-making of the organization. A group begins the work by brainstorming recent events that occurred, programs that were launched, or policies that were approved. Participants are asked to sort their observations into the following categories: risk taking, initiating, adapting, adjusting, or maintaining. Once the lists have been generated, participants are asked to name the core values expressed through the examples in each category.[7]

Each of these approaches to discerning the core values of a congregation will help constituents make meaning and clarify purpose. What is important about our past? What is the best from our past that we will carry into the future?

Living from the Core

Values and action don't always connect, particularly in liminal seasons when anxiety is heightened and people may not be living as their best selves. When values don't match action, people get confused about their purpose. Edgar Schein writes about the difference between the values we espouse and those we enact. Espoused values are the explicitly stated principles and norms that the organization claims for itself, the values we want others to believe we abide by. Enacted values are the beliefs and norms demonstrated by our constituents daily. When espoused and enacted values don't align, we have an integrity gap.

An illustration of the disconnect between espoused and enacted values is the now defunct energy corporation Enron. In 2001, the company went bankrupt after an accounting scam that involved unreported losses, well-hidden through deceitful accounting practices. Ironically, the core values touted by senior leaders at the time of the bankruptcy included respect and integrity.

In liminal seasons it is important for leaders to tend the gap between espoused and enacted values. The leader can adopt a wondering stance about the integrity gap. "We have a stated core value of _____, what do you suppose that requires of us right now?" or "Why are we choosing to do _____ right now, when our core values suggest that we ought to be doing _____?"

Orchard Lake Church espouses the value of hospitality, and in some ways, they enact that value. They post greeters in the parking lot and at every stage of entry into the sanctuary on Sunday mornings. They follow specific rituals for welcoming newcomers, which include a follow-up call from a member of the welcome team, who delivers a fresh baked loaf of bread. Everyone wears nametags and the congregation eagerly greets first-time attenders.

However, hospitality breaks down soon after the first point of contact. After worship, members gather in their own friendship groups, and newcomers stand awkwardly by, with no one to talk to. Classes and small groups are cliquish. The closeness that long-tenured members feel toward one another isn't extended to the newcomer. Hospitality isn't on the radar of most congregants.

When a congregation isn't acting out its espoused values, the gap is generally due to unstated assumptions held by constituents, unexplored assumptions that are at odds with the stated value. Surfacing and challenging unstated assumptions is core to reconciling behaviors and belief.[8]

For example, Orchard Lake Church leaders have identified two unstated assumptions that get in the way of hospitality. First, church members assume that the best way to assimilate newcomers is to get them to serve on a committee or board. You join the church and then you sign up to serve on a committee. This is how longer-term members found authentic relationship when they joined the church. Members assume that if someone has been invited to serve on a board or committee, hospitality has been extended. The rest is up to the newcomer.

Is it wrong for members of Orchard Lake Church to hold this assumption? Perhaps not. Encouraging people to participate in the leadership structure of the church is a good thing. However, if assimilation is dependent on board or committee participation, then members are withholding hospitality from those who won't or can't serve in this way.

Leaders identified a second problematic assumption. "Somebody else" is responsible for hospitality. The average person sitting in the pew doesn't see a connection between his or her behavior and the welcome experience of the newcomer. He or she believes that his or her responsibility is limited to warmly greeting the newcomer in worship. Beyond that, he or she assumes that the staff of the church and the welcome team bear responsibility for extending the hospitality of the church.

The integrity gap around hospitality at Orchard Lake will not be resolved until members articulate and adjust their assumptions. Leaders can't do this work on behalf of the people, but they can frame the work that needs to be done and invite others into the work.

Values-Based Decision-Making

We can't simply teach our core values to leaders and hope that those values will somehow infuse the choices that our leaders make. We must design decision-making and discernment processes that attend to our core values.

The first step in group decision-making involves framing the issue or problem to be addressed. The second step is to name the core values that are relevant to the decision at hand. Which values are most important, which are of lesser importance? Later in the decision-making process, when a group is evaluating possible options, each option is evaluated against the relevant values that have been named (see chapter 4 for more about this process).

Let's revisit our earlier core values example from United Church. Imagine that leaders are redesigning the small group ministry of the congregation. Leaders hope that every member of the congregation will become part of a small group, so that lasting and authentic relationships are formed in the church.

United Church is considering a partnership with a parachurch organization that designs small group ministries. Leaders are attracted to the clarity and simplicity of the approach offered by this organization. They are on the verge of signing a contract, but something is holding them back.

Leaders pause to examine the congregation's core values, to consider which of their values are relevant to the selection of a small group model.

They determine that the following two values should ground their decision-making:

> *Every Person Matters:* Each person is created in the image of God, endowed with creativity, and entrusted with spiritual gifts. We are each called to make a unique and humble contribution to the world.
>
> *Taking the Next Step:* Discipleship is a journey, an ongoing pilgrimage that begins where we are. We are guided through each stage of the journey by Scripture, the Holy Spirit, and engagement in community.

Considering these values, leaders decide that the small group model at United Church must have customizable features. If each person matters, then the United Church approach to small groups must be adaptable to honor the distinct needs and belief systems of the individual. Furthermore, if United Church is committed to meeting each person where he or she is in his or her journey, then a small group model must offer various options for different levels of spiritual maturity, life experience, and biblical knowledge.

The small group model advocated by this outside organization is formulaic. Participants are taught a shared language for talking about matters of faith. All small groups must follow identical operating principles. Every participant, regardless of biblical knowledge or spiritual maturity, is required to return to square one to learn the basic language of faith formation that this program advocates.

Ultimately, United Church leaders rejected the small group ministry model under consideration. The fundamental approach of the program was at odds with the core values of the congregation. Leaders moved on to consider other more appropriate options.

WHAT ARE WE CALLED TO DO NEXT? (EXPLORING PURPOSE)

Purpose connects us to the *why* that lies beyond our comfort and security zone. With clarity of purpose, hope grows and eventually courage emerges. Courageous people are willing to let go of the old order to discover the new. In clarifying the purpose of a liminal organization, we ask, "What purpose is worth the risk that a leader is asking people to take?"

The purpose that an organization articulates must bridge the gap between the broad aspirations of the congregation's mission and the activities of daily life. "We are called to live the love of Christ" is a beautiful aspiration. It may be necessary to state this so that we all understand why we are here. Aspirational statements provide motivation for people who are seeking spiritual meaning. However, aspirational statements present targets that are much too big. They won't significantly impact daily activities.

Author and church consultant Gil Rendle writes that people need a proximate purpose: the next appropriate piece of work, the next necessary difference that a person or people believe God seeks in their lives or in their community. A proximate purpose will encourage people to walk to the end of the beam of light cast by the flashlight they are holding, in order to cast the beam just a little further, to see an additional fragment of the way ahead. In this way people can negotiate their way to their larger aspirational purpose.[9] In liminal seasons, when we can't visualize our destination, proximate purpose is more useful than aspirational purpose. Clarity of focus about our next few steps is more important than a fuzzy picture of an unrecognizable destination.

In the early part of his career, Mohandas Gandhi returned to his Indian homeland after the successful launch of his career in South Africa. Intending to become involved in politics, Gandhi first took an extended tour through India to listen to the peasants and observe their surroundings. Toward the end of this tour, Gandhi attended a political rally where speakers were calling for home rule and expulsion of the British. The gathered crowd was largely in agreement with the principles of home rule. When the unpretentious Gandhi was finally called to the podium to speak, people began to wander around the convention floor. No one seemed particularly interested in hearing what the soft-spoken stranger had to say.

The opening of Gandhi's speech was low key. He affirmed the principles behind home rule. But then he began to argue that the issue facing India was not about home rule. The citizens of India did not really care who was ruling the country. What they cared most about was bread and salt. The convention hall began to pay attention, and by the end of Gandhi's speech the people were mesmerized. Gandhi was vocalizing what few others had managed to understand. He grounded a higher-order aspiration (home rule) in a practical reality, in the felt needs of the people (bread and salt).[10] He clarified the proximate purpose.

A leader in a liminal season must delve into the soul of the institution and touch issues of bread and salt. A purpose is credible because people can see that it is not a castle in the air, but grounded in their lived experience. It is rooted in the emotional facts of their current situation.[11]

Negotiating Competing Commitments

At any point in time, a variety of purposes and priorities exist within an organization. Private purposes may overshadow the public purpose of the institution. For example, the public purpose may be "Serving Christ by cultivating inclusion" but the private purpose is "let's just keep everybody happy and avoid conflict." The private purposes tend to serve the needs and preference of the strongest constituencies within the institution. Private purposes tend to emphasize maintenance of the status quo, security, and comfort.[12]

As a result, the priorities expressed by the board may not align with the priorities of the staff team. The priorities of the average person sitting in the pews may have little to do with the priorities of either the board or the staff. The purpose of the leader may be something altogether different from any of those listed. The leader's job is to invite reconciliation of these purposes so that they do not cancel one another out and to help the organization focus on a proximate purpose that provides energy and focus.

St. Pauls' Church has a *rich* music program—in every sense of that word. The church has an impressive pipe organ that is the envy of the community. The church boasts of five exceptional choirs, several of which tour regularly in Europe. The youth program of the church is structured around participation in the choir, and it involves an annual musical production that rivals the local community theater. The music budget is underwritten entirely by an endowment fund, and the endowed funds are restricted for use only by the music department. The size of the music department budget is as big as the operating budget for the entire rest of the church.

The music program has been slowly diminishing in quality and impact over the past decade. New families joining the church are no longer interested in having their children join the choirs. The problem is that there isn't a youth program aside from the music ministry. All of youth ministry, including confirmation, is tied to the musical life of the church.

Leaders have been advocating for the redesign of the youth program, to create something that isn't entirely music centered. To support this effort, the senior pastor keeps emphasizing a central identity statement of the church, "No matter, who you are, or where you are on life's journey, you are always welcome here." He points out that the present design of the youth program excludes young people who are not musically inclined. This argument falls on deaf ears, because a competing purpose of the church is to "Embrace excellence in music and the arts." Presently, the "excellence in music" purpose overshadows the "inclusion" purpose, simply because of resources. Likely, as long as the music department has sole access to the endowment money, their purpose will remain the penultimate purpose of the congregation.

Finding a good proximate purpose (our next best step) is key to overriding or reconciling other competing purposes. A good proximate purpose lies at the intersection of identity, context, and values. When our passions, skills, and gifts are deployed in service to a clearly defined target community, an organization that works at this intersection will find energy and create focus.

A congregation may cast a wide net and call all of its activity purposeful. Anything that falls under the umbrella of the congregation's mission qualifies as purposeful work. In the image on the next page, purposeful work is

Purposeful Work

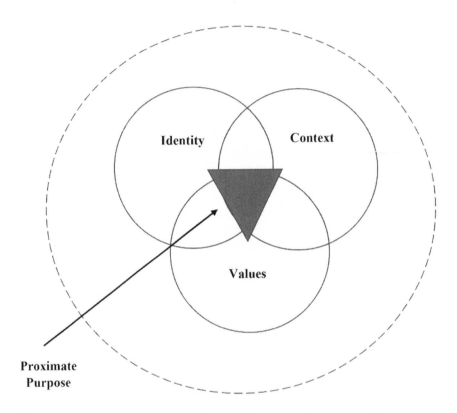

represented by the space enclosed within the circular dotted line. In most congregations, anything that involves education, stewardship, worship, service, fellowship, or outreach will fall somewhere within the circle of purposeful work. Most of the competing purposes at work in a congregation will fall under the heading of purposeful work. However, most congregations don't have adequate resources to impact every part of the circle. We cannot pursue all of our competing purposes.

Congregations are most energized when they invest their limited resources in the small triangle of space that resides at the intersection of the three smaller circles: Identity, Context, and Values. An ideal proximate purpose is one that clearly captures our emerging identity, that addresses the context of our ministry now, and that honors the core values of our organization now.

When competing purposes arise within the organization, we can negotiate our way to a proximate purpose by determining which of our possible options fall within the triangle. Of course, this requires constituents who have enough spiritual maturity and self-awareness to be reflective about identity, context, values, and competing purposes. That's a big assumption, I know.

Two of the anecdotes used earlier in this chapter demonstrate this kind of leadership awareness. The Broadstreet Church discovered a strong proximate purpose when they embraced all-abilities inclusion ministry. The church embraced a new identity when members with special needs and gifts began showing up. The congregation's context was redefined as they encountered more families within their reach that had special needs. Leaders discovered a whole new constituency they had previously ignored. Finally, the core values of the congregation emphasized inclusion and the value of every person. An all-abilities inclusion ministry at Broadstreet clearly qualifies as a good proximate purpose for this congregation, because it lives at the intersection of their identity, context, and values.

Similarly, St. Mark's discovered a new proximate purpose when they yielded to a shift in their identity. Leaders recognized that they had become a minority congregation in a multi-cultural community. When they learned more about how their context was changing, leaders identified more useful ways to interact with their community. Furthermore, the core values of the congregation emphasized "the importance of education in shaping disciples." Designing and facilitating educational venues for advancing intercultural awareness is a natural proximate purpose for this congregation.

William Hutchinson Murray, Scottish mountain climber and author, wrote, "Concerning all acts of initiative and creation, there is one elementary truth the ignorance of which kills countless ideas and splendid plans: that the moment one definitely commits oneself, then providence moves too."[13] When congregations learn to live at the intersection of identity, context, and values, remarkable synergies emerge. Resources appear. Talent emerges. New constituents join the stream of energy.

Pitfalls to Avoid

There are two major pitfalls that church leaders should avoid when helping a congregation clarify its purpose: pursuing growth for growth's sake and adopting generic revitalization programs because they worked someplace else.

Today, many congregations are panicked about numerical decline. Numerical growth has become the penultimate purpose, because congregations believe that growth will ensure their survival. When asked what their purpose is in this season, leaders may respond with, "We just need to grow."

Hoping for growth is not a purpose, it is a desired outcome—attached to an unarticulated purpose. I have never seen a church grow simply because members wished for growth. Truthfully, most growth aspirations stem from constituents wanting more people, just like themselves, to help support the budget and existing programming. I have only seen churches actually grow in response to the pursuit of authentic ministry that served a contextual need. Chasing growth for the sake of growth is a knee-jerk reaction that lets a congregation avoid the hard work of clarifying identity, context, and values. It compels leaders to jump on everyone else's bandwagon, chasing flavor-of-the-month programs that worked well elsewhere, but may have little to offer this institution.

All healthy organizations are growing in some capacity. A congregation that is not growing is dying. However, growth won't necessarily be reflected numerically. It doesn't have to involve more bodies in worship or in membership, or more dollars in the budget. It should involve growth related to the congregation's proximate purpose: deepening spiritual practices, integrating kids with special needs into the life of the congregation, strengthening intergenerational connections, and the like.

A leader trying to move an organization away from general aspirations about growth, toward a more specific purpose, can ask these questions. Growth to what end; what will growth accomplish that is central to our mission? Who will benefit from growth? Is growth possible or even desirable? Where will growth come from?[14]

Today, many congregations are pursuing prepackaged revitalization programs. Any resource that begins with "five easy steps to . . ." or "six essential elements of . . ." appeals to the false self of the institution. We would all like to believe that there are magic pills available to fix our ills. Many acclaimed programs were developed because a specific methodology worked well in some context. However, canned programs ignore congregational identity, context, and values. The program worked well in another context because it honored the identity, context, and values of the original host institution. Success in one context doesn't guarantee an authentic fit elsewhere.

At the end of the day, discovering our next best step, our proximate purpose, won't magically resolve liminality. We will still be disoriented. We still won't have clarity about our ultimate destiny. However, we will have created enough energy and focus to continue building the bridge as we walk on it.

NOTES

1. Margaret J. Wheatley, *Who Do We Choose to Be? Facing Reality, Claiming Leadership, Restoring Sanity* (Oakland, CA: Berrett-Koehler Publishers, Inc., 2017), 293–94.

2. Margaret Silf, *The Other Side of Chaos: Breaking through When Life Is Breaking Down* (London: Darton, Longman and Todd Ltd., 2011), 35–36.

3. C. Otto Scharmer, *The Essentials of Theory U: Core Principles and Applications* (Oakland, CA: Berrett-Koehler Publishers, Inc., 2018), 60–61.

4. Frederick Buechner, *Wishful Thinking: A Theological ABC* (New York: Harper Collins, 1973).

5. Edgar H. Schein, *Organizational Culture and Leadership* (fourth edition) (San Francisco, CA: John Wiley & Sons, 2010), 26.

6. Various techniques for reviewing the history of the congregation in a group context can be found in Gil Rendle and Alice Mann, *Holy Conversations: Strategic Planning as a Spiritual Practice for Congregations* (Lanham, MD: Rowman & Littlefield, 2003), 262–63.

7. Lawrence L. Lippitt, *Preferred Futuring: Envision the Future You Want and Unleash the Energy to Get There* (San Francisco, CA: Berrett-Koehler Publishers, Inc., 1998), 53–54.

8. Schein, *Organizational Culture and Leadership*, 27–32.

9. Gil Rendle, *Quietly Courageous: Leading the Church in a Changing World* (Lanham, MD: Rowman & Littlefield, 2019), 230.

10. Robert E. Quinn, *Building the Bridge as You Walk on It: A Guide for Leading Change* (San Francisco, CA: Jossey-Bass, 2004), 136–37.

11. Quinn, *Building the Bridge*, 138.

12. Rendle, *Quietly Courageous*, 229.

13. William Hutchinson Murray, *The Scottish Himalayan Expedition* (London, UK: Dent, 1951).

14. Ronald Heifetz, Alexander Grashow, and Marty Linsky, *The Practice of Adaptive Leadership: Tools and Tactics for Changing Your Organization and the World* (Boston, MA: Harvard Business Press, 2009), 38.

Chapter Seven

Engaging Emergence

Are We There Yet?

Chaos is found in greatest abundance wherever order is being sought.
—Terry Pratchett, *Interesting Times*

A five-acre wooded plot rests quietly at a busy intersection near my home. Thousands of cars pass by on an average day, few if any slowing to consider the significance of the woods.

To the random observer, little occurs in the woods for fifty-one weeks of every year. Then, for one week in late October, the woods serve as temporary home to an unruly flock of blackbirds, thousands of them embarking on their annual migration to someplace warm.

During that week, the average passerby wouldn't notice anything amiss in the daytime woods. When the birds rest during the day, each claims an individual spot on a naked tree branch, and nothing looks out of the ordinary. It's a different story at dusk when the sun begins its gentle descent below the horizon.

Something in the setting of the sun triggers a magnificent response among the birds, as if they have been charged with heralding the setting of the sun to those of us who move about blissfully unaware. At dusk, the birds rise in a singular windswept movement, like the unfurling of a flag. Without fanfare, the undisciplined birds transform into a fluid swarm, rising into the air, folding inside and out, shifting shape and form, but always maintaining the integrity of the flock.

A collective wisdom seems to birth the rising. There are no apparent leaders guiding the swarm. The gathered flock rises with elegant synchronicity. For twenty minutes, the birds dance like a well-orchestrated ballet company, before losing their flocking impulse and settling in for the night.

It is a beautiful and frightening event to witness. Sometimes, when I have forgotten the blackbirds' existence from one year to the next, the arrival of the flock unsettles me. Their sudden appearance as a swarm, just at the edge of my field of vision, is an eerie reminder of an Alfred Hitchcock thriller. I nervously check my windows and doors to make certain that I am safely separated from the birds, even as I long to soar among them. The flock appears wild and out of control. Their numbers remind me of my own insignificance, and I am painfully aware that if they wanted to inflict harm, they certainly could.

The wild and beautiful swarming of the blackbirds is an illustration of emergent behavior, when many simple entities operate independently in a chaotic environment, forming more complex behaviors collectively.

In human organizations, emergence is a naturally occurring pattern of change that happens over time when a group interacts in conditions of upheaval, disturbance, or dissonance. Eventually, novel and coherent structures arise in response to changes in the environment. A moment arises when disorder gives way to new order. Something fresh emerges—a higher order pattern, a decision, a new structure, or a change of direction.

Organizations will always gravitate toward spontaneous order over meaningless chaos.[1] No organization lives indefinitely in the chaos of a liminal state. Either the organization will cohere around a new organizing principle, or it will eventually die. Liminality will find resolution.

Order arises when a galvanizing idea or principle is introduced and group behaviors begin to cohere around that idea. Individual agents act and react to the actions of those around them until a meaningful organizing pattern emerges. In organizations, this often happens with unexpected, almost magical leaps of intuition.

Let's consider a simple example. A group of volunteers gather on a Saturday morning to clean up the grounds of their beloved church building. A harsh winter has left the grounds cluttered with random garbage and natural debris fit for the compost pile. Each volunteer arrives with a cup of coffee in hand, tools from home, and random ideas about how the grounds ought to look and how the cleanup process ought to unfold. As the volunteers gather, there is excitement in the air, coupled with chaos around competing ideas for how to organize.

Members of the cleanup crew argue among themselves for a while, until someone observes three core activities that are central to the work: trash removal, pruning, and planting. Participants adopt this organizing scheme and begin sorting themselves into three teams, each volunteer gravitating toward a team based on personal preference. Each team designs its own workflow. A new work order emerges out of the earlier confusion. Volunteers rally around coordinated action that isn't led or supervised. Activity at the micro level (in this case, volunteers identifying their work) coalesces into macro-level behavior (a functioning cleanup crew.)

Organizational chaos during liminal seasons is unsettling. Anxiety levels are high when something has ended and constituents are waiting for new order to arise. Followers often turn on their authority figures when anxiety peaks. "Why aren't you resolving this ambiguity for us? Aren't we paying you to lead us out of this mess? Don't you have any ideas about what should happen next?"

Authority figures are often hooked by these expectations and scurry about trying to restore order and resolve chaos. They step in to manage the chaos as a way of demonstrating their leadership competency. In liminal seasons, the temptation to resolve chaos by restoring the status quo is seductive. Leaders think, "Let's just bring back something that feels familiar to people, so they will calm down."

We are like Aaron, who faced a grumbling group of Israelites when Moses disappeared atop Mount Sinai. This newly formed community, which just days before had agreed not to worship false gods, begged for a golden calf they could worship. Aaron embraced the hero's role by resolving the chaos, restoring the status quo, and giving the people what they wanted. He resolved their disorientation by giving them their calf. Unfortunately, it was the wrong move for the community.

In a liminal season, the only way forward is through the uncertainty and chaos. The leader's challenge is not to eliminate the ambiguity and chaos, but to embrace emergence—and stand with people during their confusion.

Herein lies the struggle. Emergence is not a controlled process that can be led by an authority figure. It is a self-organizing process that feeds on experimentation, risk-taking, and learning from failure. It is messy and anxiety producing. Emergence doesn't happen through the clearly articulated vision of a leader, followed by the careful execution of goals and action plans. In fact, these traditional leadership activities may very well squelch emergence.

Emergence is fundamentally leaderless activity. It cannot be orchestrated or managed. However, there are things that a leader can do to support emergence as it unfolds. This chapter will help the reader understand the natural cycle of emergence and discover a meaningful leadership supporting role.

EMERGENCE AS NATURAL ORDER

Let's return to the swarming behavior of the blackbirds. Scientists studying the flocking habits of birds have used computer modeling to track these movements. Apparently, three very simple rules govern the flight pattern of each bird within the swarm. The collective result is called murmuration. The process is elegantly simple, as only nature could devise. These are the three rules:

1. Rule of Separation: Avoid crowding your neighbor. The principle is referred to as short-range repulsion. Every bird demonstrates a respect for the bubble of space between itself and its neighbor.
2. Rule of Cohesion: Stay close to your neighbor. Never allow too much space to emerge between you and your closest flying companion. Always seek to move toward another bird.
3. Rule of Alignment: Steer toward the average heading of your six closest neighbors. The swarm is not led. There is no centralized decision-making. The practice of steering in accordance with the movement of your closest neighbors is what keeps the flock aligned.[2]

These three principles guide the formation of the swarm. Each bird manages its own relationship to the others, honoring these impulses. The result is a synchronous show of nature that is both practical and awe-inspiring. Flocking behavior is not just for show; it serves a useful purpose for the birds. Some scientists believe that the flocking impulse occurs at dusk to generate collective warmth and to exchange information about good feeding areas before settling in for the evening.

Murmuration is the result of micro-level behavior adopted by each bird in the flock which produces a macro-level property—the swarm. A higher level of complexity emerges that no one planned or led. We see this kind of behavior all throughout God's created order. We find examples of emergence in the physical sciences, social sciences, philosophy, systems theory, and art. Ants and bees create colonies, fractal patterns generate crystals and snowflakes, urbanites create neighborhoods, and spectators create stadium waves.

Consider the increasing use of traffic circles, or roundabouts, to accommodate traffic flow at busy intersections. At first glance, the roundabout appears to invite chaos when compared to the traditional stop sign or traffic light. Cars are moving in all directions without clear right of way. In fact, roundabouts have been proven to reduce accidents and to improve the flow of traffic. They rely on a simple "yield-at-entry" rule in which approaching vehicles must wait for a gap in the circulating flow before entering the circle. The cars in the circle have right of way over the cars that have not yet entered. Traffic circles encourage slower speeds and greater awareness of surroundings, which accounts for their safety. This is emergence, collective order arising naturally out of chaos with the imposition of a few basic rules.

How many of you are screaming at the page right now, "But I hate driving through traffic circles! The chaos is unnerving." Exactly. Welcome to emergence.

EMERGENCE IN ORGANIZATIONS

Emergence in organizations follows an observable and predictable cycle. It begins with the ending of something that used to work but doesn't work any longer. The ending of the status quo produces chaos. The organization enters a liminal, disorienting state where individuals must experiment and learn from their failures. Eventually, group learning occurs and new structures and behaviors more suitable for a new chapter emerge. When we understand how the pattern flows, we are better able to recognize where we are in the unfolding of events, and we can encourage more productive work at each stage of the journey.[3] Here's the process in a nutshell:

1. A *disturbance* of the status quo occurs, but the organization tries to ignore or deny the disharmony to preserve the status quo.
2. *Disruption* occurs. The disturbance becomes bothersome to the point where it can no longer be ignored. The status quo becomes unbalanced, and structures and processes begin to disintegrate.
3. We embrace *innovation*, discovering new practices to resolve the disharmony, in accordance with our core identity, strengths, and values.
4. We find *coherence*, learning how to integrate what is novel into what is already known.

Engaging emergence is difficult for all involved, but especially difficult for the authority figure "in charge." The authority figure at the helm of an organization engaging emergence must lead with presence. A leader who is invested in knowing, advocating, and striving will have difficulty embracing emergence. The leader who practices unknowing, attending, and surrender will rest more productively into the cycle. (Stop and read chapter 2 if you are reading this book out of order.)

WELCOMING DISTURBANCE

Ralph Waldo Emerson once said, "People wish to be settled; only as far as they are unsettled is there any hope for them."[4] The process of emergence begins when something disharmonious, something unsettling, occurs inside or outside of the organization, but the organization tries to ignore or deny the disturbance to preserve the status quo.

One of the most common disturbances to the status quo is a budget crisis—not enough money in the budget to pay our staff or not enough money to maintain or restore our building. Other examples of disturbance may include an inability to recruit new volunteers, the departure of a staff member, or a change in a zoning ordinance that impacts how we manage our property.

The natural human response is to minimize disturbance and to restore the equilibrium. So we work to raise more money, or we enter a "faith and hope" line item in our budget. We postpone necessary maintenance on the building. We beg long-suffering volunteers to serve just one more term. We dip into our endowment to pay for the staff team that we can no longer afford.

It is hard to invite people to see a disturbance as an invitation to adaptation. Organizations move around a center or equilibrium, a steady state, much the way the planets revolve around the sun. We learn certain ways of being together and getting things done. We share basic assumptions, and we hold shared practices that keep things stable.

Social psychologist Kurt Lewin identified two sets of opposing forces that keep organizations in this state of equilibrium. At any point, driving forces are pushing us away from our equilibrium and toward something new, and restraining forces are keeping us firmly entrenched in our status quo. [5]

Consider the simple example of sitting in the chair that is supporting you right now. The force of gravity is pushing you downward, so that you don't float up into the atmosphere. At the same time, another force is resisting the pull of gravity, so that you don't collapse to the ground. That opposing force is the resistance of the chair in which you are sitting. As long as gravity and the resistance offered by the chair remain in balance, you will remain seated upright—in your stable state. If either one of those forces suddenly shifts, you will find yourself moving through space, either to the ground beneath you or into the air, depending upon which force is strongest.

Organizations are under the continual influence of both driving and restraining forces. Adaptation beckons us forward, but restraining forces keep us in our place.

A congregation gathers at 8:30 and 10:00 a.m. on Sunday mornings for worship and has met at those times for decades. No one remembers any longer why those two time slots were initially chosen. For a while, leaders have been entertaining the notion of moving worship times to 9:00 and 11:00. On each occasion when the subject is raised, various constituent groups raise concerns about the change.

The driving forces supporting the change (a move away from the status quo) include more readily available nursery workers at the later hours, the strong personal preferences of families with children who long for different worship times, the possibility of creating a shared faith formation hour between services, and the perception that millennials would prefer a later worship hour.

However, several strong restraining forces stand in opposition to the change and support the status quo. These forces include the long-established Sunday morning habits of members, the strong support for an 8:30 start among congregants over seventy years of age, and city-wide parking fees that kick in at 11:30 a.m. on Sunday mornings, inhibiting a later start time.

To unfreeze (disrupt) the system and make way for adaptation, the balance between the forces that maintain the status quo must be upset. The driving forces must become stronger than the restraining forces. This may happen through intentional or accidental strengthening of the existing driving forces, adding additional driving forces, or reducing/eliminating restraining forces. In short, the social equilibrium must be disturbed.

If large numbers of younger families begin leaving the congregation to attend a cross-town congregation with worship times more conducive to their needs, this would strengthen a driving force for change. Or if one or more of the restraining forces were reduced, we might witness a similar shift. Imagine, for example, that the city suddenly made parking free all day on Sunday in every lot surrounding the church, so there was no longer a parking fee during the proposed later service. The status quo equilibrium would be suddenly disturbed because of shifts in the environment.

During liminal seasons, the status quo naturally destabilizes. As the old-world order gives way, the driving and restraining forces that have maintained equilibrium shift. As leaders, our challenge is to work with this natural disorientation to invite something transforming. Or we may even encourage destabilization by adding to the driving forces or eliminating restraining forces. We may participate in the demise of the status quo.

Unfortunately, the knee-jerk reaction of many leaders is to restore the status quo in response to rising anxiety. We seek to calm things down. Our followers question our efficacy when we stand back and let a disturbance fester, or when we actively participate in the deconstruction.

Authority figures are expected to provide direction, protection, and order for their constituents. Organizations look to their authority figures to define problems and provide solutions, to protect people from external threats, and to restore order by reinforcing norms and roles. Leaders are rewarded for resolving disturbances and restoring the status quo. Anxiety is reduced when disturbances are quickly resolved.[6]

However, the leader who calms the disturbance and restores the status quo may be squelching adaptation. Organizations adapt when they yield to disturbance. "What if we let this fall apart; let's see what might happen next." When we take a step back and invite disruption, we also open ourselves to innovation. Innovation eventually leads to coherence and a new macro order.

As an analogy, consider the simple process of cooking noodles in a pot. Gently boiling water transforms the dried noodles into something edible through the chemistry of applied heat. Too little heat and the water will not boil. The noodles remain hard and inedible. Too much heat produces a rapidly boiling pot that expels or burns the noodles as the pot boils over. Good cooking requires a slow and steady heat source. Organizational transformation also requires a slow and steady heat source.

In an organization, disturbance is the heat source. Something stops working or falls apart and we don't jump in to fix it. The driving and restraining sources that maintain the status quo shift, throwing the organization out of equilibrium. If the authority figure quickly extinguishes the heat by restoring the status quo, there is no adaptation. If the authority figure allows the forces to shift too quickly, we experience the equivalent of the pot boiling over. Conflict levels rise, people begin to leave the organization, or they reject the leader because the disorientation becomes intolerable.

Liminal leaders must learn to manage the heat of disturbance. Heifetz refers to this skill as sustaining the *productive zone of disequilibrium*.[7] We must let the disturbance provoke, prod, and disorient. Let the flickering ember get some air so that it fans into a productive flame. During emergence, effective leaders allow themselves and others to be bothered without letting anxiety rise to highly uncomfortable levels. They resist the compulsion to restore the status quo; they yield to the emerging disorientation.

DISRUPTING COHERENCE WHILE STAYING ALIVE

Eventually, a disturbance becomes bothersome to the point that it can no longer be ignored. The endowment fund can no longer make up for the budget deficit. The postponed maintenance on the building results in the boiler exploding. Volunteers don't step forward to staff the dysfunctional committee. Disturbance gives way to disruption, which occurs when we discover how the status quo is failing us. We cannot ignore the disturbance and survive. Structures and processes quit working, and systems that once sustained us begin to disintegrate.

It isn't enough to simply manage a disruption. Leaders must monitor the anxiety, helping followers embrace disorientation at a tolerable pace. The anxiety of followers will rise and fall as constancy gives way to disruption.

At times, leaders may need to provoke disorientation because followers are too complacent with the status quo. People are ignoring the disturbance to their own peril and the leader must heighten their attention and dissatisfaction. At other times, leaders must settle things down a bit, because the dissonance has grown too strong and threatening.

Jerry is a new region minister. He oversees the joint ministry efforts of 160 congregations. The region Jerry serves can no longer afford to do things as they have always been done. The region downsized its staff from ten people to six people in the five years prior to Jerry's hire. However, no efforts have been made to redefine the work of the region to accommodate the reduction in staff. Pastors, congregational leaders, and the region board still expect the same level of ministry engagement and the same kind of relationships with staff that they had when the staff was nearly twice its current size.

Jerry knows his task is to help the region get clarity about its core purpose and to streamline structure and process to better serve that purpose. The region is firmly attached to its decades-old model of ministry. They want a region staff that resources search and call, resources and equips local congregations, resolves church conflicts, coaches individual pastors, and leads coordinated mission efforts. Jerry knows that he and his staff can no longer satisfy all these expectations. He's not even sure that it would be in anyone's best interest for his staff to do so, even if the region could afford it.

The budget crisis is a disturbance that the region has been minimizing for years by trying to deliver the same services with fewer resources, and they are not maintaining the status quo well. The ongoing reduction of staff has been uncomfortable, but region leaders have diminished the impact of the deficit by working harder with less. Jerry intuitively knows that his job is to invite the region into the next stage of emergence. He must allow the budget crisis to fully unfold, so that structures begin to fail. Only then will the region discover an innovative pathway forward. The trouble is that people are going to attack Jerry's leadership when he does this.

What skills must Jerry use to nurture this upheaval? He will need to figure out how to provoke dissatisfaction, destabilize existing structures, and act politically—all the while instilling confidence in his own authority to keep on leading.

Provoke Dissatisfaction

Ending the status quo means allowing dissatisfaction to ferment—not with the leader, but with some part of the organization. The simplest and easiest way for a leader to provoke dissatisfaction is to tell the truth—unvarnished, unspun, and to the point. Humans are easily tempted to minimize or bury hard truths. We reveal the budget deficit, but then we quickly reassure constituents by emphasizing all the positive things that are happening. We downplay the crack in the foundation by covering it up with a pleasant looking rug.

Tell the truth and tell it masterfully. Craft a message so people see how their typical behavior leads to failure. Show them how continuing the status quo is threatening the values they cherish most.

Author, pastor, and Christian missiologist Ed Stetzer wrote an article for the *Washington Post* titled, "If It Doesn't Stem Its Decline, Mainline Protestantism Has Just 23 Easters Left."[8] Bold and to the point, Stetzer's article provokes a reaction. He roots his observations in a central practice of the Christian tradition, the celebration of Easter, and he predicts its demise. He shocks his readers out of their complacency by pointing to current trend lines and boldly predicting a doomed future.

Another way to provoke dissatisfaction is to surface competing commitments. The leader can name the values that the organization promotes and illustrate how the status quo requires us to favor one of those values to the exclusion of the other.

> We say we are interested in reaching parents with young children. Our present worship schedule accommodates the preferences of many who already call this community home. However, our research shows that families with small children (our target population) want to worship at _____ time. Are we more committed to the preferences of our existing members or the needs of those who don't currently attend because of our worship time? Can we experiment and find a way to satisfy both sets of needs?

When people acknowledge competing commitments, they are more likely to let go of stability, to discover new ways to satisfy more of what we value.

We also provoke dissatisfaction when we allow dissenting opinions to be heard. Every organization is host to naysayers. These are the people who provoke a silent groan when they stand to speak. The "problem" person(s) that the organization has learned to ignore because of their chronic dissension, or because they are fixated on a single solution. "We wouldn't be having problems with worship attendance if we would just had a better organ."

Dissent is critical to originality and creative thinking. Minority viewpoints are important because they stimulate divergent thought. Even when those divergent opinions are wrong, they fuel the creative thought process of others in the room.[9] They contribute to the generation of ideas. Dissenting opinions build dissatisfaction with the status quo.

So, instead of minimizing or ignoring the dissenting voice, the leader can amplify that voice through active listening. If the dissenter doesn't articulate his viewpoint well, the leader can rephrase what the dissenter has said so that it is palatable to the ears of listeners. Get them thinking about the ideas behind the dissenting voice. Invite curiosity about the dissatisfying defaults people have clung to, and then invite people to be courageous enough to consider alternatives. "I wonder when and why we first began doing X. Is there some reason we couldn't do Y instead?"

Jerry engages a combination of these tactics. First, he prepares a projected financial statement that shows the region's insolvency within ten years, without a change of direction. Then he gives the dissenting voice of a board member more air time. One unpopular member of the board has been advocating for the sale of the region office building. Other board members find her advocacy tiring. Jerry doesn't agree with her ideas, but he gives the board member space on the agenda to express her ideas, so that others will begin thinking more creatively about alternative solutions. Finally, Jerry inserts his own pondering questions into board conversations, "Why are we doing it this way? Do you suppose a different way of doing this might serve us better now?"

At times, people grow weary of Jerry's provocations and the airspace he gives to "problem" people. Nevertheless, Jerry persists. When anxiety grows to intolerable levels, Jerry backs off for a while to let things calm down. Then he begins again. Finally, region leaders and constituents yield to the disruption; they acknowledge the need for adaptation and change.

Throughout this process, Jerry's leadership abilities are often under attack. His constituents wonder if he knows what he is doing, if he has control of the situation. Jerry must hold steady in the face of criticism. He must learn not to personalize the critique of his leadership. He must stay the course. His approval ratings will likely rise again once the system finds its new equilibrium. In the meantime, leading the region won't feel particularly rewarding.

Destabilize Structures

Organizational structures provide stability and create predictability. Organizational charts, job descriptions, policy statements, and charters define how things get done. They create boundaries that minimize disruption and foster efficiency.

As the cycle of emergence unfolds, structure gives way to anti-structure, so a higher order, a better way of approaching things, can unfold. We must let existing structures, policies, and programs destabilize, so they can crumble when constituents are ready, and make way for a new thing.

People grow anxious when the predictable structures give way. Anxious people go to incredible lengths to restore the status quo and minimize their own anxiety. Anxious people tend to behave badly. And when they do, a leader's energy is often directed at coping with the dysfunctional behavior of a few, rather than focusing on the health of the whole. An effective leader resists being drawn into the dysfunction and remains focused on health and hope.

Management and training consultant Peggy Holman talks about the destabilizing process as a drive for differentiation.[10] The whole breaks apart into its distinct parts before reorganizing into something new. Think of atoms bonded together to form molecules. When the status quo destabilizes, the whole separates into individual, distinct parts. The atoms break free and exhibit their own unique properties for a time before rejoining other atoms to form new molecules. The moment when atoms break free is ripe with potential and possibility. What will emerge next?

Destabilization can be thought of as creative destruction. Within organizations, individuals are suddenly unleashed and free to participate in the life of the organization in new ways. Power and authority structures rearrange. Voices that were once marginalized are suddenly attended to. Voices that once wielded considerable influence are less regarded. People discover new and creative ways to engage ministry with one another.

The region staffing structure that Jerry inherited served the old way of doing things. Jerry supervises two associate region ministers (ARMs). The two associate roles are still functioning as they did when the region had resources to employ five ARMs. The ARMs have traditionally been generalists, meaning five associate ministers each provided all region services for a geographical district, each with thirty-some churches. The generalist ARM role no longer works. Two associates cannot provide generalist coverage to seventy-five congregations apiece.

The staffing structure is clearly broken. It is clear to Jerry that the traditional ARM role must die. There is one major stumbling block to moving forward—Craig, one of the two remaining associates. Craig has a fifteen-year history in the role and has developed a tight relationship with his original district of thirty-five churches. Craig has convinced his original district churches that they couldn't possibly thrive without the traditional ARM role—without him. Craig has offered every possible resistance to the redefinition of his role. Craig's district is also the most resource rich of the five districts, which fuels his power base.

Jerry would like to begin a staff restructuring but knows that Craig and "his" churches will continue to resist. Craig is three to five years away from retirement, but Jerry knows that the region doesn't have the resources to wait this one out.

Instead of addressing Craig's resistance directly, Jerry destabilizes the region structure in a different way. A neighboring region has experienced many of the same budget and infrastructure issues. Jerry and the other region minister have been quietly exploring the possibility of a merger, a consolidation of the two regions. Jerry decides that it is time to go public with the merger conversation. Jerry brings the idea to his board and gets permission to form a taskforce. The taskforce is charged with evaluating merger and reorganization possibilities.

Jerry is not married to the idea of the merger. He maintains a wondering stance—"not knowing" which structure is best for the future of the region. He encourages the most forward thinkers in the region to volunteer for the taskforce. Craig and his inside group of supporters are not invited onto the taskforce.

The merger conversation is destabilizing. Previous conversations about restructuring the region staff had ground to a halt over the role of the ACMs. People simply weren't ready to let go of the ACM as liaison between the region and the church. When Jerry let that non-productive conversation die and introduced the possibility of merger instead, things began to destabilize in more helpful ways.

First, Craig saw the writing on the wall. It became evident that his role was going to substantially change—one way or another. Craig abruptly announced his retirement. Leaders felt free to imagine new possibilities. The merger conversation also helped people shift away from a geography-centric understanding of region life and began imagining other network configurations. Perhaps churches could be grouped according to size, ministry emphasis, or theological orientation.

In the end, the region chose not to merge with its neighbor. Instead, it created a nimbler board, staff, and committee structure. The merger conversation served as a meaningful container for dialogue about core purpose that the region needed to have. It provoked creative destruction of the status quo. It allowed chaos to emerge at a pace that people could tolerate.

When Jerry entered merger conversations with a neighboring region, he exceeded the assigned authority of his role. He did not have a legitimate right to enter this conversation on behalf of his region. Jerry was careful to keep these early conversations confidential until he was clear that his region leaders were ready to consider the possibility of merger. In these very early stages, Jerry had many "off the record" conversations with key stakeholders in the region whose support would be needed should the conversation move forward.

Jerry stepped back inside of his authority limits when he brought the merger conversation to his board and asked for their approval to appoint a taskforce. He let others nominate members of the taskforce, but Jerry worked carefully behind the scenes to ensure that healthy players were in the conversation. He used his veto power to prevent a dysfunctional constituent from being appointed to the taskforce. He made certain that healthy dissenters had conversations with the taskforce so that their voices and concerns were heard. In short, Jerry operated as a savvy political agent in his own region. He was wise as a serpent, but as gentle as a dove (Matthew 10:16).

Once Craig announced his retirement from the ACM role, Jerry immediately scheduled a series of listening sessions with the leaders from Jerry's district. He wanted to hear their reservations first hand, and he wanted to reassure district leaders that they had a hope-filled future.

Jerry's leadership was challenged throughout the process. Many people were unhappy with Jerry's approach, but at the end of the day Jerry survived the creative destruction process. More than that, Jerry became a beloved leader on the other side of the reorganization. People grew to appreciate his bold leadership and his demonstrated commitment to the region and its people.

FOSTERING INNOVATION

Eventually, out of disturbance and disruption, the seeds of a new beginning surface. The first shoots that appear in the spring garden are unrecognizable as the full plants they will become. Likewise, the first signs of innovation are unrecognizable as a solution to disorientation.

Innovation is the practice of designing or discovering new practices that will eventually usher in a new organizing principle. Innovation rarely occurs in a linear manner. It cannot be managed according to timelines and calendars. Rather, innovation is a messy and iterative process that needs to be protected and nurtured.

Innovation relies on the presence of diversity. Albert Einstein is quoted as saying, "We can't solve problems by using the same kind of thinking we used when we created them." Innovation rarely emerges from the center of an organization, from the core group of authority figures who are thinking and acting on behalf of the whole organization. Rather, innovative thinking generally emerges from the edges of the organization, among those who are thinking differently about the challenges, and those who are not encumbered with daily decision-making.

Innovation begins with curiosity, with a sense of awe and wonder about the state of the organization. Inviting wonder unleashes brain power, enhances generosity, and stimulates creativity. Innovation grows out of experimentation, and it happens naturally when we empower people to solve problems that they care about.

Experimentation and Risk-Taking

An effective leader notices where experimentation and risk-taking are occurring, inside or outside of the organization. They provide an umbrella of protection for innovative ideas to germinate and grow before they are brought into the central life of the organization. Sometimes, ignoring a creative experiment for a short period of time is the best thing that a leader can do. Paying attention too early on will draw too much attention to a fledgling idea that needs more time to take flight.

An innovative leader encourages experimentation. Emergence depends upon continuous learning. We foster ongoing experiments, we pause to learn from our mistakes, we adapt and offer new iterations. Running many small experiments with minimal risk is better than taking on a few big risks. Small experiments provide more opportunities for learning and rapid course correction.

Experimentation happens best under conditions of random encounter, when diverse people have open encounters with one another. When we increase the opportunities for connection, interdependence, and interaction, we elicit new ways of thinking and behaving.[11]

Group dialogue processes like Appreciative Inquiry, Open Space Technology, and World Café are highly effective tools for inviting this kind of interaction. In these forums, members of the organization come together in atypical group formations to listen to one another more deeply and to explore new ways of seeing the organization and the present challenges.

A leader must foster a propensity for action in the organization. This is challenging because organizations that have been disrupted are often fearful, and when people are fearful, they become more passive. The leader must draw constituents out of their passivity.

Experimentation and learning happen best when we invite people to take responsibility for what they love about the organization and to act where they feel most passionate and engaged. Too often, congregations fill volunteer slates based on organizational polity and traditionally defined needs. "We need five new deacons, three new elders, and two trustees, because that's what our by-laws say. Who will volunteer to serve?"

One of the blessings of disorientation and disruption is that the old structures disintegrate. This frees constituents to participate in undefined ways. We don't agonize over unfilled positions but let those positions remain unoccupied to see what emerges in response to the vacancy. Instead of begging people to staff our Sunday school, we imagine an alternative educational model that requires fewer volunteers. We invite people to say "yes" to emerging opportunities that stimulate their imaginations and their impulse to serve. If the disturbance over unfilled roles becomes worrisome enough, it helps the organization begin to discover what is most important and what it is willing to let go of.

Innovation happens naturally when we empower people to solve problems they care about, when we let go of our obsessions with right order and proper channels, and when we let everyone have equal access to information and communication channels. When we let go of our need to feel in control of what happens next, remarkable things begin to occur.

Embracing Failure

We encourage risk-taking and experimentation when we embrace failure as a learning opportunity. Failing forward is a critical skill in nurturing emergence.

Congregations are biased toward action. We plan, we act, and then we plan and act some more. We don't stop to honestly assess progress. When we fail, we don't stop to figure out what we can learn from the failure. Our default is to put a positive spin on the failed attempt and to quickly move on to the next action. Over time, this creates an operating culture that fears failure. We fear investing our diminishing resources in something that may not succeed, and ultimately our risk-taking and experimentation grind to a halt. We choose slow death over deep change because we haven't learned to fail well. [12]

It is helpful to think about failure as a necessary consequence of innovation. Failure is inevitable when we are doing something new and unexpected. What we know from science is that every outcome is equally important when testing a hypothesis. With every outcome we learn what doesn't work, which means we are one step closer to discovering what might. [13]

We learn from failure when we integrate action with careful reflection. Before an experiment begins, leaders must be clear about the changed condition they hope to produce, along with the targeted intervention, and the resources that are available for investment. A hypothesis or assumption must be named. Leaders need to determine what measures will be used to determine success or failure. At the end of each experiment, lessons learned must be claimed. What turned out to be true/false? What errors were made? Is it worth repeating in some modified way—or is the experiment over? The following case illustrates how one very traditional, dying congregation did just that.

First Baptist: Engaging Emergence

First Baptist Church (FBC) boasts of a rich, 180-year history. Built on the inside perimeter of a historic town square, the FBC steeple is an iconic symbol in the community. For much of its history, FBC has been known as an anchor church in the community and in the denomination.

Sadly, the past fifty years at FBC have been marked by decline. Like many older, downtown churches, declining attendance and growing operating deficits brought the church to the brink of closure two years ago. The gathered worshipping community now averages fifty participants, most over the age of sixty-five. The church is struggling to maintain the magnificent building that was once the hallmark of its existence.

Leaders explored selling the building outright. However, deed restrictions on the land prohibit the use of the building for anything other than a church. Furthermore, the community regularly hosts concerts in the sanctuary because of the church's world-class pipe organ. Community leaders are encouraging church leaders to find some productive use of the building that will ensure it remains an open and vibrant presence on the square.

After exploring several merger possibilities that didn't pan out, the leaders of the congregation decided to simply get curious about what might be possible. They wondered what the building required of them, asking themselves, "What would the building say to us, if it could speak, about this next era of ministry at First Baptist?"

Out of this wondering stance, the pastor of FBC made a bold proposal to the governing board:

> The church is operating at an annual $30,000 deficit. We have $300,000 remaining in our endowment fund, which can be used to cover our operating deficits, so long as the money lasts. What if we use that money to foster innovation, seeking to learn what we can about the connection between our building and the community. Let's conduct a series of experiments with our remaining money, rather than limping along and spending down the endowment until our death. If we die more quickly because of the risks we take, so be it. At least we will have been faithful to our heritage and our call.

Board leaders rallied around the pastor's call to innovation. Church leaders knew that the present members didn't have the energy or the imagination to innovate. So they advertised for part-time mission interns who would pursue bold experiments on behalf of the congregation. Each intern would design an experiment targeted at connecting the building with the needs of the community. Each intern would be paid ten hours per week for one year to foster a ministry dream of his or her own imagining. At the end of one year, church leaders would evaluate ministry results and reimagine the church's relationship to its building and its future.

An innovation team of seven church leaders, including the pastor, was formed. The purpose of this team was to oversee the selection of interns, evaluate progress, consolidate learning, and keep the board and the congregation engaged in the learning process.

The team advertised for their interns on the local Craigslist. The requirements listed in the ad were simple. "Present us with an idea that you are passionate about pursuing, that makes use of our building, and serves the community. Our selected interns will resonate with this statement: Let my heart be broken by the things that break the heart of Christ."[14]

The team met with anyone who responded to the ad. Initially, some of the ideas were poorly formed, but the experiments sharpened in scope and focus as the team and intern candidates continued in dialogue. Several candidates dropped out as the process unfolded, because their initial ideas didn't hold up under scrutiny. The team used the five core values of the congregation to evaluate whether the experiments were a good fit for FBC.

Eventually, the team selected six mission interns, each offering a bold idea that created opportunities for innovation and learning, each embracing one or more of the congregation's core values. The interns met monthly with the innovation team to process results and to foster learning. They met weekly as a small group with the pastor for support and to discover points of emerging connectivity. The following experiments were undertaken.

1. The Garden: Lisa and Sarah were friends with a passion for raw food and a concern about the limited availability of healthy food choices within urban communities. Their hearts were grieved when they witnessed local retailers discarding good produce that was just a little beyond its prime, while neighboring residents went hungry.

   Sarah had a passion for vegan cooking. She wanted to sponsor a weekly free Vegan Feast at the church, using expired produce collected from local food retailers and some of the produce from the hydroponic garden.

   Lisa's dream was to establish a hydroponic garden in several of the unused classrooms of the church building. The produce grown in the garden would be used to support the Vegan Feast and to stock several local food pantries.

   In the early days of this experiment, a community of sixty-five people, including twenty-five children, quickly formed to celebrate a weekly meal together. After several months, the worshipping community of the church joined with the Vegan Feast at a monthly open-air worship experience in the park across the street from the church.

2. A Free Health Clinic: Chioma was a young woman from Nigeria, pursuing a master's degree in public health at a nearby university. Chioma stepped forward to lay the groundwork for a free health clinic operating out of the church building. Early efforts to launch the clinic were encouraging, but within the first six months, all planning folded under intense political pressure from a few local organizations that didn't want a free health clinic operating on the town square. Opponents feared the type of people that a free clinic might attract onto the town square.

3. Seeking Beauty: A recently retired minister with a passion for photography birthed a weekly program at the church to engage impoverished members of the community through the arts.

   Each week, one low-income family was selected to work with the intern, taking photographs of things that the chosen family found beautiful in their local context. Each week, the homeless community was invited into the building to engage in an hour of respite, engaging the artistry of the week, playing games, and enjoying food together.

   Seventy people initially enrolled to participate in this experiment. However, the experiment quickly floundered. Members of the targeted community simply didn't have the planning, time management, and follow-through life skills to make the program viable.

4. Multi-Cultural Children's Center: A local Hindu woman, originally from Nepal, brought her dream of a program that connected children and families through play and art. Using the FBC building as her base, she formed a weekly place for play and interaction that connected

families across cultures and faith traditions. This program experienced modest success. Thirty to forty people participated regularly, although the program struggled continually because of the poor English-speaking skills of its coordinator. Several of the people who participated in this program also connected to the Vegan Feast.

5. Refugee Outreach: Emily, a local college freshman, had just completed a one-month mission trip serving in a Syrian refugee camp when she saw the Craigslist ad. Emily had a passion for serving resettled refugees trying to set up new households with limited resources. Her dream was to form a furniture collection and refinishing site to support refugee families. Emily was granted a section of the church basement to pursue her dream, and the furniture donations began pouring in.

   Emily's energy and passion were contagious. She easily fulfilled her goal of refinishing, repurposing, and distributing one hundred pieces of furniture. She eventually went on to establish five other collection sites. Within the first year, for practicality purposes, the site at FBC was relocated and consolidated into one of the other sites. Emily's project spun off into its own non-profit enterprise.

6. Ducks in a Row: Chris was a free-spirited young man who lived near the church. He was raising ducks. Chris noticed how frightened urban children were when they encountered the ducks, because of the little exposure the children had to live animals. His dream was to develop a program of urban animal husbandry that allowed children in impoverished neighborhoods to come into regular contact with farm animals. He located his offices (not the animals) in the church building.

   Unfortunately, Chris's personal life was in chaos for most of the internship year. He never managed to get a meaningful program off the ground and the year ended before he had anything productive to show for his efforts.

The innovation team worked hard to be permission giving about the use of the building, to stay connected with the interns, and to engage the congregation in the learning process. It was hard. Innovation team members were often discouraged by the congregation's lack of interest in the experiments. First and foremost, congregants wanted assurance that their pastoral care and worship needs would be met. As long as these conditions were maintained, the congregants seemed willing to tolerate the experiments. Most showed little interest in the learning process. Nevertheless, the innovation team pressed forward.

Midway through the year of innovation, it appeared that several of the intern experiments might help with church revitalization. Several of the ventures looked like they might evolve into long-term ministries of the church.

At a minimum, several landlord/tenant arrangements appeared viable. And then, over the span of a few more months, a crisis emerged in each program, and all but one of the experiments closed. At the end of the first year, only the hydroponic garden/Vegan Feast remained, and its viability wasn't certain.

At first, the innovation team was devastated. It appeared they had nothing to show for their year of experimentation. The church had used its scarce resources to no end. But then, the pastor and the transitions team began to focus on what they had learned. They paid attention to emerging patterns and surprising findings. We will hear more about their learning and their next steps in later paragraphs, but first we need to better understand coherence.

FINDING COHERENCE

Perhaps you have seen a spiral wishing well at your local science center or museum. The well demonstrates funnel physics. An observer drops a penny into the outer bowl of a funnel-shaped plastic mold. The penny begins a slow, irregular elliptical journey around the outer edge of the funnel, wobbling in orbit around a hole at the center of the funnel. Each time the penny appears to lose momentum and falter, the penny drops into a lower orbit closer to the center of the funnel. With each drop, the penny's orbit around the center of the funnel tightens and becomes more regular, until finally the coin descends the nearly vertical walls of the funnel.

This phenomenon is like the momentum we observe during innovation. At first, our experiments feel random, ponderous, and disconnected. We wonder if we are in fact accomplishing anything significant. Over time, as we learn from our mistakes, our actions grow increasingly focused. Our experiments become more purposeful and begin to coalesce into something meaningful. A clustering of viable options arises. It happens not through the reassembly of old broken parts, nor through the reconstruction of what once was. In unpredictable ways, random interactions begin to converge into new structures and processes. Chaos resolves itself. We have found coherence.[15]

There are things a leader can do to nurture coherence. The leader may focus the attention of the organization by clarifying what is arising. The leader can distinguish between meaningless repetition and life-giving iteration. And finally, the leader can wait to act until discovering simplicity on the other side of complexity.

Clarifying What Is Arising

As we wait for coherence to emerge, it is helpful to clarify the intentions behind our experiments. The seeming randomness of experimentation leaves people in the organization feeling unmoored. What are we trying to accomplish? What, if anything, do we still stand for? What are we in pursuit of?

The nature of emergence is such that we can't point to expected outcomes. We know only that we are in pursuit of a new chapter, a reconfigured way of living out our mission and purpose. However, we can remain crystal clear about our intention. We can talk about what matters most to us, our purpose and vocation. We can talk about the core values that continue to drive our mission and ministry (see chapter 6).

As FBC allowed its ministry interns to experiment on behalf of the congregation, members predictably grumbled about the exercise. "This seems like one giant waste of resources. What, exactly, do we think we are learning?"

The pastor repeatedly articulated the overarching purpose of the experiment. "We are trying to discover a new relationship between the congregation, the building, and the community. We are making decisions about what we will and will not do, based on the five core values that we articulated last year."

Clarifying also involves naming what is arising. FBC leaders made some shared observations. "The Vegan Feast seems to resonate with our value of inclusion and our delight in community. We enjoy the intergenerational energy that the children's center has brought back to our building." And, "During our work with the refugee community, we discovered that there are hundreds of churches and non-profits in our community that all focus on the needs of the poor. No one is coordinating the efforts of those non-profits."

Naming something into being is a sacred act. Moses stood at the edge of the promised land and retold the people their story. He named them as the people of the covenant, God's chosen nation. He linked their past with their present and their future. This is what effective leaders do. They tell the story as it unfolds. They imagine a hope-filled future based on what is being learned right now. They name what is emerging by integrating unfolding action into the core identity of the people (see chapter 5).

In *Theory U*, Otto Scharmer refers to this process as "letting go and letting come." Letting come is the flipside of intention. We set our intention and then yield to what the universe brings to us next. We follow a trail of experimentation and unfolding to see where we are led. We pay attention to what is emerging from our inner source of knowing. Letting go of old assumptions and presuppositions. Tapping into the learning and leading that comes to us from the future.[16]

In *Engaging Emergence*, Peggy Holman frames numerous possibility-oriented questions that can help an organization clarify what is arising.[17] Here are some of the most poignant:

- What do we wish to conserve?

- What do we want more of?
- What keeps us going?
- What guides us when we don't know?
- What question, if asked and answered, would make a difference in this situation?
- What can we do together that none of us could do alone?
- How do we steward what is arising?
- Given what has happened, what is possible next?

In response to these questions, FBC saw that the community needed its building on the square as much as, or maybe even more than, the congregation needed it. Congregants had always thought of the building as theirs to occupy and manage. Lately, they had come to regard the building as their burden to bear. Now they were beginning to see the building as a resource for the community—a gathering and coordinating space for non-profits. They were also coming to realize that perhaps the congregation only needed to be a tenant in the building, not its owner/manager. But who would the owner/manager be if it was not the congregation?

Repetition versus Iteration

Mark Twain is reputed to have said, "History doesn't repeat itself, but it rhymes."[18] What we have experienced in the past is likely to repeat itself, but never identically. Unfortunately, communities of faith often behave as if past experiences are naturally repetitive. "Our attendance was much higher when we advertised in the yellow pages. We should advertise in the yellow pages again." In liminal seasons we need to learn new responses to changing conditions. Instead of repeating the past, we must iterate.

Repetition is the recurrence of the same action or event in response to a stimulus. Repetition is static. If I do X, it will result in Y. Unfortunately, repetition doesn't yield much learning. That truth is captured in Einstein's saying: "The definition of insanity is doing the same thing over and over again but expecting different results."

Iteration also involves doing something again and again. However, in iteration each new act is influenced by the previous experience and slightly adapted to learn something more. We focus on incorporating the learning from the previous experiment and integrating what is novel into what is known.[19]

At FBC, several of the intern experiments failed within months. Some members wondered if the church should start up new intern projects to replace the failed experiments. However, leaders decided that it didn't make sense to go back and start brand new random experiments. The church was learning new things as the experiments unfolded, even as they failed. They didn't want to keep repeating the same part of the experiment over and over. They were more interested in discovering the next chapter based on what they were learning.

Waiting for Simplicity to Emerge

In organizations, emergence typically involves an intuitive leap in practice, a major disruption from the past. Months or years of small incremental changes often follow an initial, large disruption, much like the outward ripples that occur in a pond after the initial disturbance that produces a splash. These smaller, incremental changes strengthen coherence.

For the leader, it can be difficult to discern whether to attend to the initial splash or to wait and respond later when the subsequent ripples have worked their way outward. It is tempting to imagine that the initial splash is the thing to respond to, a clear resolution of our liminal state. When that large discontinuous interruption occurs, we want to jump on board and declare that a new beginning is upon us.

It is generally better, though, to wait and attend to the subsequent ripples before declaring coherence. As the subsequent ripples dissipate, true simplicity emerges. Prior to that, the waters are muddied by complexity.

At FBC, the pastor felt a lot of pressure to declare an early victory. The early successes of "The Garden" and the "Children's Center" were temptations to declare an end to the experiment. Church leaders wanted to embrace their new tenants and claim a permanent resolution to the building crisis.

Unfortunately, coherence was not yet at hand. Only one of the original experiments ultimately proved viable. After the big splash of the intern experiments was over, the ripples of learning continued.

What emerged was the need for a collaborative venue in the community. Each of the ministry intern projects had focused on some aspect of battling poverty. The weekly and monthly meetings with interns made church leaders aware of the vast number of organizations in the community that already focused on poverty—over eight hundred, in fact. Over and over, the interns bumped up against the competing needs and redundant offerings of these sister organizations.

The intern experiment birthed an important insight: the building on the square could serve as a coordinating space for non-profits addressing poverty. This idea aligned well with a long-standing core value of the congregation: "We will battle poverty by fostering self-respect and self-determination among the impoverished."

However, it was also becoming increasingly clear that the management and maintenance of the building was beyond the scope of the congregation's current energy and resources. What began to coalesce was the need for a new organizational construct.

A new round of experimentation began. FBC became an instrumental partner in founding an advocacy coalition. The coalition was formed for the express purpose of bringing residents and non-profit organizations together to cooperate in alleviating poverty in the community. An independent governing board was formed through the coordinated efforts of community leaders and church leaders. A guiding principle was that the church building on the square would eventually be deeded to the advocacy coalition, with the congregation remaining in place as a tenant of the coalition.

The formation of the coalition seems rather far removed from the original intern experiment. Numerous attempts at innovation occurred. There was confusion and failure along the way. In the end, the coalition was a rather simple and elegant "solution" to the problem of "What shall we do with our building?" The congregation couldn't arrive at the simple solution without first wading through the incredible complexity of disturbance, disruption, experimentation, and iteration.

Today, the FBC building houses the activity of more than twenty non-profits. The congregation is working toward transferring ownership of the building over to the coalition. The church will continue to reside in the building as a tenant. The congregation is in many ways doing well, although not yet thriving. Membership has not grown much larger than it was at the beginning of the intern experiment, although the congregation has grown younger, with 30 percent of its members having joined in the last three years. The long-term viability of the congregation remains unclear. What is clear is the congregation's ongoing commitment to serving the community and battling poverty.

No organization is static. Structures and processes emerge, evolve, and decline. We have been conditioned to think of the decline of an organization as a failure, rather than as a naturally occurring season in the cycle of emergence. Our effectiveness as leaders is not determined by whether an organization grows on our watch. Our effectiveness will ultimately be judged by the extent to which we attend to disorientation, embrace disruption, support innovation, and nurture coherence. The cycle of emergence takes a long time. Many of us will finish our tenures or even our careers before the organizations we are leading will find their way to new forms of coherence. This does not mean that we have failed. Our task is to tend the garden so that others may harvest what we have tended.

A FINAL WORD

God's people have grappled with liminality since the beginning of recorded history. Eras end and people endure extended periods of disorientation while they wait to discover a way forward. This phenomenon is not uniquely ours.

In the book of Ezra, we read the story of the Jewish nation finding its way back to Jerusalem after a period of exile. The first temple, and the accompanying way of life that supported the temple, is gone. However, the foundation for a new temple is being laid, and the people gather to celebrate this important new start for the community. This is how the Hebrew scriptures describe the gathering:

> And all the people gave a great shout of praise to the Lord, because the foundation of the house of the Lord was laid. [12]But many of the older priests and Levites and family heads, who had seen the former temple, wept aloud when they saw the foundation of this temple being laid, while many others shouted for joy. [13]No one could distinguish the sound of the shouts of joy from the sound of weeping, because the people made so much noise. And the sound was heard far away. (Ezra 3:11–13)

Leaders in liminal seasons must endure and interpret a lot of noise. There are those who long to go backward, to a more stable time reminiscent of former glory eras. Others want nothing more than to forge ahead and discover their new beginning. Few want to live in the disorientation of the middle stage, the liminal state where nothing feels resolved. And yet, the liminal season, ripe with possibility for learning and growth is exactly where we need to be.

Like those early Jews, we need leaders who can stand with people in their liminal state, leaders who can negotiate the noise, offer reassurance and hope, and gently guide the community toward the work that is theirs to do. The work is difficult, but also exciting. We stand on the frontlines, waiting and watching to see what God will do next. We can take comfort and reassurance from these words from Deuteronomy 31:6, "Be strong and courageous. Do not fear or be in dread of them, for it is the Lord your God who goes with you. God will not leave you or forsake you."

NOTES

1. Peggy Holman, *Engaging Emergence: Turning Upheaval into Opportunity* (San Francisco: Berrett-Koehler Publishers, Inc., 2010), 18.

2. https://en.wikipedia.org/wiki/Flocking_(behavior). Accessed on May 10, 2017.

3. These stages are adapted from "The prime innovation pattern" as described by Peter J. Denning and Robert Dunham in their book, *The Innovator's Way: Essential Practices for Successful Innovation* (Cambridge, MA: The MIT Press), 25.

4. Ralph Waldo Emerson, "Circles," in *Essays and Lectures* (New York: Library of America, 1983), 413.

5. Kurt Lewin, *Resolving Social Conflicts and Field Theory in Social Science* (Washington, DC: American Psychological Association, 1997), 47.

6. Ronald Heifetz, Alexander Grashow, and Marty Linksy, *The Practice of Adaptive Leadership: Tools and Tactics for Changing Your Organization and the World* (Cambridge, MA: Harvard Business Press, 2009), 28–29.

7. Heifetz, Grashow, and Linksy, *The Practice of Adaptive Leadership*, 28–31.

8. Ed Stetzer, "If It Doesn't Stem Its Decline, Mainline Protestantism Has Just 23 Easters Left," *The Washington Post*, April 28, 2017. https://www.washingtonpost.com/news/acts-of-faith/wp/2017/04/28/if-it-doesnt-stem-its-decline-mainline-protestantism-has-just-23-easters-left/?utm_term=.5042a7b6e1ba.

9. Adam Grant, *Originals: How Non-Conformists Move the World* (New York: Viking Press, 2016), 185.

10. Holman, *Engaging Emergence*, 3.

11. Grant, *Originals*, 7.

12. Robert E. Quinn, *Building the Bridge As You Walk On It: A Guide for Leading Change* (San Francisco, CA: Jossey-Bass, 2004), 97–98.

13. Ed Catmull and Amy Wallace, *Creativity, Inc.: Overcoming the Unseen Forces that Stand in the Way of True Inspiration* (New York: Random House, 2014).

14. International missionary Bob Pierce wrote these now-famous words in his Bible after visiting suffering children on the Korean island of Koje-do. This impassioned prayer is what guided him as he founded and led the ministry of Samaritan's Purse in 1970.

15. Holman, *Engaging Emergence*, 171–72.

16. C. Otto Scharmer, *Theory U: Leading from the Future as It Emerges* (second edition) (Oakland, CA: Berrett-Koehler Publishers, Inc. 2009), 195–96.

17. Holman, *Engaging Emergence*, 194–99.

18. There is no evidence to suggest that Mark Twain ever used this phrase, despite the fact that it is frequently attributed to him. Twain did use the phrase "History never repeats itself" in a novel he co-wrote with his neighbor Charles Dudley Warner, the 1874 edition of *The Gilded Age: A Tale of To-Day*.

19. Holman, *Engaging Emergence*, 101–5.

Bibliography

Adichie, Chimamanda. "The Danger of a Single Story." Online video clip. TED talks. Recorded July 2009.

Bacik, James. "Thomas Merton on the True Self." *June Reflections* 38, no. 10 (2015).

Barry, William S.J. *Paying Attention to God: Discernment in Prayer.* Notre Dame, IN: Ave Maria Press, 1990.

Barton, Ruth Haley. *Pursuing God's Will Together: A Discernment Practice for Leadership Groups.* Downers Grove, IL: InterVarsity Press, 2012.

Boorsteing, Michelle. "Acts of Faith." *The Washington Post.* April 6, 2016.

Bourgeault, Cynthia. "Four Voices Method of Discernment." *Contemplative Journal* May–June 2015.

Bourgeault, Cynthia. *Relearning Surrender.* Victoria, BC: The Contemplative Society, 2012.

Branson, Mark Lau. *Memories, Hopes, and Conversations: Appreciative Inquiry, Missional Engagement, and Congregational Change.* Lanham, MD: Rowman & Littlefield Publishing Group, Inc., 2016.

Bridges, William. *Managing Transitions: Making the Most of Change* (third edition). Philadelphia, PA: DeCapo Press, 2009.

Buechner, Frederick. *Wishful Thinking: A Theological ABC.* New York: Harper Collins, 1973.

Butler Bass, Diana. *Grounded: Finding God in the World—A Spiritual Revolution.* New York: Harper Collins, 2015.

Catmull, Ed, and Amy Wallace. *Creativity, Inc.: Overcoming the Unseen Forces that Stand in the Way of True Inspiration.* New York: Random House, 2014.

Cooperrider, David, Diana Whitney, and Jacqueline Stavos. *Appreciative Inquiry Handbook: The First in a Series of AI Workbooks for Leaders of Change.* San Francisco, CA: Berrett-Koehler Publishers, Inc., 2005.

Curtiss, Victoria G. *Guidelines for Communal Discernment.* Louisville, KY: Presbyterian Church [USA].

Denning, Peter J., and Robert Dunham. *The Innovator's Way: Essential Practices for Successful Innovation.* Cambridge, MA: The MIT Press.

Dressler, Larry. *Consensus through Conversation: How to Achieve High-Commitment Decisions.* San Francisco, CA: Berrett-Koehler, 2006.

Edwards, Tilden. *Embracing the Call to Spiritual Depth: Gifts for Contemplative Living.* New Jersey: Paulist Press, 2010.

Emerson, Ralph Waldo. "Circles." In *Essays and Lectures.* New York: Library of America, 1983.

Grant, Adam. *Originals: How Non-Conformists Move the World.* New York: Viking Press, 2016.

Green, Thomas H. *Weeds Among the Wheat: Discernment—Where Prayer and Action Meet.* Notre Dame, IN: Ave Maria Press, 1984.

Heifetz, Ronald, Alexander Grashow, and Marty Linsky. *The Practice of Adaptive Leadership: Tools and Tactics for Changing Your Organization and the World.* Boston, MA: Harvard Business Press, 2009.

Heifetz, Ronald A., and Marty Linsky. *Leadership on the Line: Staying Alive through the Dangers of Leading.* Boston, MA: Harvard Business Press, 2002.

Hester, Richard L., and Kelli Walker-Jones. *Know Your Story and Lead with It: The Power of Narrative in Clergy Leadership.* Herndon, VA: The Alban Institute, 2009.

Hillman, James. *The Soul's Code: In Search of Character and Calling.* New York: Random House, 1996.

Holman, Peggy. *Engaging Emergence: Turning Upheaval into Opportunity.* San Francisco: Berrett-Koehler Publishers, Inc., 2010.

Huddleston, Mary Anne. *Springs of Spirituality.* Ligouri, MO: Triumph Books,1995.

La Shure, Charles. "What Is Liminality?" *Histories and Theories of Intermedia* October 18, 2005.

Lewin, Kurt. *Resolving Social Conflicts and Field Theory in Social Science.* Washington, DC: American Psychological Association, 1997.

Lippitt, Lawrence L. *Preferred Futuring: Envision the Future You Want and Unleash the Energy to Get There.* San Francisco, CA: Berrett-Koehler Publishers, Inc., 1998.

Mann, Alice. *Can Our Church Live? Redeveloping Congregations in Decline.* Bethesda, MD: Alban Institute, 1999.

May, Gerald C. *The Dark Night of the Soul: A Psychiatrist Explores the Connection Between Darkness and Spiritual Growth.* New York: Harper Collins, 2005.

Merton, Thomas. *New Seeds of Contemplation.* Boston, MA: Shambhala Publications, 2003.

Morris, Danny E., and Charles M. Olsen. *Discerning God's Will Together: A Spiritual Practice for the Church.* Nashville, TN: Alban Books, by an arrangement with Upper Room Books, 1997.

Mostyn, John H. "Transforming Institutions: God's Call—A Director's Response." In *Tending the Holy: Spiritual Direction Across Traditions*, edited by Norvene Vest. New York: Morehouse Publishing, 2003.

Murray, William Hutchinson. *The Scottish Himalayan Expedition.* London, UK: Dent, 1951.

Neuhauser, Peg C. *Corporate Legends and Lore: The Power of Storytelling as a Management Tool.* Austin, TX: PCN Associates, 1993.

Newell, John Philip. *Celtic Prayers from Iona.* New York: Paulist Press, 1997.

Palmer, Parker. *A Hidden Wholeness.* San Francisco, CA: Jossey-Bass—A Wiley Imprint, 2004.

Quinn, Robert E. *Building the Bridge as You Walk on It: A Guide for Leading Change.* San Francisco, CA: Jossey-Bass, 2004.

Rendle, Gil. "Narrative Leadership and Renewed Congregational Identity." In *Finding Our Story: Narrative Leadership and Congregational Change*, edited by Larry A. Golemon. Herndon, VA: Alban Books, 2010.

Rendle, Gil. *Quietly Courageous: Leading the Church in a Changing World.* Lanham, MD: Rowman & Littlefield, 2019.

Rendle, Gil, and Alice Mann. *Holy Conversations: Strategic Planning as a Spiritual Practice for Congregations.* Lanham, MD: Rowman & Littlefield, 2003.

Rohr, Richard. *Everything Belongs: The Gift of Contemplative Prayer.* New York: The Crossroad Publishing Company, 1999.

Rohr, Richard. *The Naked Now: Learning to See as the Mystics See.* New York: The Crossroads Publishing Company, 2009.

Rohr, Richard. "The Dualistic Mind." *The Center for Action and Contemplation Newsletter.* January 29, 2017.

Rohr, Richard. "What Sustains Me: Contemplation." *Sojourners.* June 15, 2009.

Rothauge, Arlin J. *The Life Cycle in Congregations: A Process of Natural Creation and an Opportunity for New Creation.* Congregational Development Series. New York: Episcopal Church Center, 1994.

Saarinen, Martin F. *The Life Cycle of a Congregation.* Washington, DC: Alban Institute, 1986.

Scharmer, Claus Otto. "The Blind Spot of Leadership: Presencing as a Social Technology of Freedom." www.ottoscharmer.com/publications/articles. April 2003.

Scharmer, Claus Otto. *The Essentials of Theory U: Core Principles and Applications.* Oakland, CA: Berrett-Koehler Publishers, Inc., 2018.

Scharmer, Claus Otto. *Theory U: Leading from the Future as It Emerges* (second edition). Oakland, CA: Berrett-Koehler Publishers, 2016.

Schein, Edgar H. *Organizational Culture and Leadership* (fourth edition). San Francisco, CA: John Wiley & Sons, 2010.

Silf, Margaret. *The Other Side of Chaos: Breaking through When Life Is Breaking Down.* London: Darton, Longman and Todd Ltd., 2011.

Simmons, Annette. *The Story Factor: Inspiration, Influence, and Persuasion Through the Art of Storytelling.* New York: Perseus Books. 2009.

Sternberg, Robert J., ed. *Wisdom: Its Nature, Origins, and Development.* Cambridge: University Press, 1990.

Stetzer, Ed. "If It Doesn't Stem Its Decline, Mainline Protestant Has Just 23 Easters Left." *The Washington Post.* April 28, 2017. https://www.washingtonpost.com/news/acts-of-faith/wp/2017/04/28/if-it-doesnt-stem-its-decline-mainline-protestantism-has-just-23-easters-left/?utm_term=.5042a7b6e1ba.

Szakolczai, Arpad. "Liminality and Experience: Structuring Transitory Situations and Transformative Events. *International Political Anthropology Journal* 2, no. 1 (2009).

Thomassen, Bjorn. "Liminality." In *The Encyclopedia of Social Theory,* edited by Austin Harrington, Barbara L. Marshall, and Hans-Peter Müller. London, UK: Psychology Press, 2006.

Thomassen, Bjorn. "The Uses and Meanings of Liminality." *International Political Anthropology Journal* 2 (2009).

Tickle, Phyllis. *The Great Emergence: How Christianity Is Changing and Why.* Grand Rapids, MI: Baker Books, 2008.

Turner, Victor. "Betwixt and Between: The Liminal Period in Rites de Passage." In *The Forest of Symbols.* Ithaca, NY: Cornell University Press, 1967.

Turner, Victor. "Liminality and Communitas." In *The Ritual Process: Structure and Anti-Structure.* New York: Routledge Press, 2017.

Underhill, Evelyn. *The Ways of the Spirit.* New York: Crossroads, 1997.

Volf, Miroslav. *The End of Memory: Remembering Rightly in a Violent World.* Grand Rapids, MI: Eerdmans Publishing Company, 2006.

Ware, Corrin. *Discover Your Spiritual Type.* Lanham, MD: Rowman & Littlefield, 2014.

Wheatley, Margaret J. *Who Do We Choose to Be? Facing Reality, Claiming Leadership, Restoring Sanity.* Oakland, CA: Berrett-Koehler Publishers, Inc., 2017.

Wink, Walter. *Unmasking the Powers: The Invisible Forces That Determine Human Existence.* Philadelphia, PA: Fortress Press, 1986.

Index